HISTORICAL RAMA

D.K. HARI
D.K. HEMA HARI

Bharath Gyan Series

Original title: **Historical Rama**

First Edition: October 2010

ISBN: 978-938059219-0

Graphics, Design & Layout : Bharath Gyan Studio

Published by:

THE ART OF LIVING

Sri Sri Publications Trust
The Art of Living International Centre,
21st KM, Kanakapura Road, Udayapura, Bangalore - 560082
Email: info@srisripublications.com
Website: www.sattvastore.com
Toll Free 1800-258-8888

Contents

Benedictory Note

Gurudev Sri Sri Ravi Shankar
Founder - Art of Living

Though Ramayana has had a deep impact not only in India but in other parts of Asia and world, during the colonial rule it was brushed aside as mythology. The work of D.K. Hari and Hema in establishing **Historical Rama** is praiseworthy. What has been missing is faith free from dogma and science free from prejudice. This book is a combination of both. They have carefully studied and scientifically established the historicity of Rama. Hope this will rekindle the pride in our past and confidence in the future.

29 June, 2010

Bengaluru, India

About Bharath Gyan

Bharath Gyan has been collating specific, scientific knowledge of India, using ancient knowledge sources and modern scientific tools and methods, from a present day perspective and relevance.

The knowledge of the Indian civilization is available scattered in various forms such as books, manuscripts, oral tradition amongst scholars, various art forms, customs and traditions of the land.

The current generation is facing a barrier in reaching out to this knowledge due to the limited availability and access to such resources, the ancient languages and the style of expression used, the approach to the subjects etc., all of which are in contrast to the present day system of expression or understanding.

In Bharath Gyan, as part of our quest for the specific scientific knowledge and practices of the civilization, we have come across many stories, ideas, views, theories, factual events and statements.

With the help of traditional scholars with a modern bent of mind and modern scientists open to traditional knowledge systems, we have endeavoured to carefully sift through all this data, with an inquisitive, rational, logical and scientific mind to understand the knowledge from a fresh interdisciplinary perspective. The outcome of this analysis is the compilation of Bharath Gyan.

Over 10 years, spanning across 108 subjects, the independent facts and data collated, self validate and corroborate each other beautifully in this compilation, as pieces of a jigsaw.

Bharath Gyan, a research organization, is in the process of bringing this knowledge out through far reaching and engaging mediums so that it can be easily understood and enjoyed by all across the world.

The objective is to bring out this knowledge and wisdom, in relevance to current day topics of interest, trials and tribulations faced by Indians as well as the world.

Besides filling the readers with wonder at the not-so-commonly known scientific facets of our ancient civilization, it is hoped that this knowledge and approach of the ancients will kindle or aid future research for the benefit of science and mankind.

Can we make the past converge with the present for the future?

Ours is perhaps not the first effort in this direction, neither should it be the last ...

As one of the initiatives, Bharath Gyan, encouraged by Gurudev Sri Sri Ravi Shankar, has entered into an alliance with the Art of Living, to jointly repurpose the compiled knowledge into various knowledge products for dissemination to the community at large.

Our website www.bharathgyan.com provides more insights into our activities.

Foreword

It is a privilege to be invited to inscribe a 'Foreword' to the monumental work of Sri. D.K. Hari and Smt. D.K. Hema Hari of Bharath Gyan on **'Historical Rama'.** Ramayana is a beautiful and majestic story of great values and noble deeds. It is a representative chronicle of man's ageless and supreme struggle to preserve all that is beautiful and precious in human life. The story of Rama has been told again and again ever since the great chronicler Valmiki recorded his own contemporary eye witness account.

Jawahar Lal Nehru in his **'Autobiography'** said that in the great festive days of Dussehra and Ramlila when tableaus and processions re-enacted the old story of Ramchandra and his conquest of Lanka, crowds were attracted to Bharadwaja's Ashram where there was once a primitive University. Nehru re-calls that on those days endless stream of visitors went to their house from dawn to dusk. The Bhardwaja's ashram was close to the Nehru home.

Again in his **'Discovery of India',** he says that in Ramayana, facts and fiction are so interwoven together as to be inseparable and this *"amalgam becomes an imagined history"*. Nehru quotes Goethe who *"condemned those who said that the old Roman stories of heroism, of Lucretia and others were spurious and false. Anything that was essentially spurious could only be observed and untruthful and never beautiful and inspiring and that if the Romans were great enough to invent things like that, we at least should be great enough to believe them"*.

Nehru also refers to Michelet, the French Historian who with special reference to Ramayana said:

"Whoever has done or willed too much let him drink from this deep cup a long drought of life, of youth.....Everything is narrow in the West - Greece is small and I stifle; Judea is dry and I pant. Let me look towards lofty Asia, and the profound East for a little while. There lies my great poem, as vast as the Indian ocean, blessed, gilded with the sun, the book of divine harmony wherein there is no dissonance. A serene peace reigns there and in the midst of conflict an infinite sweetness, a boundless fraternity, which spreads over all living things as ocean (without bottom or bound) of love, of pity of clemency".

What is splendorous beyond man's imaginative capacity cannot be fictional.

Story of Rama is the splendid example. In his celebrated **"Lectures on the Ramayana"** V.S.Srinivasa Sastry observes;

"...it is no act of impiety to study the Ramayana as an epic poem concerning human beings'. It is an act, on the other hand, which gives to Valmiki his own due, establishes him as a man who held in his mind – assuming that he was the one that wrote the story – a clear, fully-formed, full-blooded conception of men and women of superior ability and superior value, of superior moral stature. I would exhort you all to read the poem from this point of view".

"You must read the story as a human story, lived among human beings by a human being, and, then, Oh, what rich treasures there are of wisdom in it".

Of course, sentimentalists felt a sense of hurt when their God was treated as a mere mortal. But then, it needed only a mortal to vanquish Ravana as he had the divine boon of protection from Gods and Demons and all others, except mere mortals. The Lord descending to a earth to extinguish a great evil, had, had to ironically act as and really believe himself to be, only an ordinary mortal, like every one else. That is why Rama himself declared *"Atmanam manusham manye".* These are all intriguing and inscrutable ways of the divine beyond the grasp of ordinary mortals.

Now to the theme of this book; Sri. D.K. Hari and Smt. D.K. Hema Hari have presented us with a massive compilation of evidence, historical, archaeological, chronology of coincidences of stellar and astronomical combinations in the major events of Rama's life and, of course, the large volume of literature in different languages repeatedly lending confirmation to historicity. The genealogical record, both of the ancestry and posterity, are overwhelmingly against any likelihood of mere imagined and concocted version. The cumulative effect of this precious evidence, amenable to cross verification, would vindicate the Book's theme.

But, we live in an age of irreverence, of cynicism and distrust which are, at least in part, manifestations of a disillusionment, characteristic of the times. The existence or non-existence of God can not be established by any length of arguments. The agnostic and the atheist are as much part of the Hindu inheritance. Heterodoxy, Charvakas, the Lokayatas are all very much part of our civilization. Valmiki himself refers to Jabali Rishi who counsels Rama against the foolishness of wallowing in sentimental renunciation of the pleasures of kingship. There can be endless argument about these matters; but there can be no argument against Faith. This work lends great credence to the faith of the faithful.

Justice M.N.Venkatachaliah
Former Chief Justice, India
Supreme Court
August 5, 2010
Bengaluru

Preface

The Authors, D.K. Hari and D.K. Hema Hari
Conceptualizers, Bharath Gyan

In recent times, there have been many a question raised on the Historicity of Rama. These came into limelight due to issues that were taken to the court regarding some of the aspects connected with Rama.

Rama, while is a divinity of millions of Hindus all over the world, has also been believed through the ages to be a historic King of India who ruled from Ayodhya. Rama is an instance where the divide between the earthly and the divine is hardly existent. It is seamlessly merged with one another, at times fixed on the real life, historical existence of Rama and at other times, transcending into the subtler realms of divinity and faith.

In the last 300 years, Rama was dismissed as a mythical figure, dismissing the ancient, traditional history of India. Ever since then, the issue of the acceptance of Rama as one of the most influential, historical king of this land, has been one of the questions in front of young India.

Two of the recent happenings in the last couple of decades, have provided just the right opportunity for analyzing and understanding the historicity of Rama.

One is the debate over Rama *Setu* or the Adam's Bridge, the structure in the sea which connects India and Sri Lanka. The debate has risen in the context of plans and efforts to break this bridge to create a shorter shipping route around India.

This bridge is believed by majority of the Indians, to be a man made bridge built during the period of Rama. Hence the demand from a majority of the public that this relic from the period of Rama should not be destroyed, as it would their hurt religious sentiments.

The debate therefore entered into the realm of discussing *"whether this structure called Adam's bridge is a natural formation or is it a manmade construction?"*, in which, different sections of the population of India, have taken different stands, ranging from pure faith to pure economics.

In this raging public debate, people have taken stances which are either black or white. This has left little option for a rational approach to understanding the historicity of Rama, since only if Rama is historical, can the bridge also be manmade.

Through this effort, we look at Rama and the *Rama Setu,* Adam's Bridge from a rational, scientific and logical perspective to try and understand historicity of Rama.

Is Rama historical?

The other debate is over a particular piece of land in Ayodhya, called through ages as *Ram Janmasthan* or the birthplace of Rama.

This debate has risen in the context of whether this particular land should be handed over to Hindus to build a temple for Rama or to the Muslims, since there was a Mosque on this land since mid 1500s.

At the bottom of the debate is also an underlying question on the historicity of Rama since only if Rama is historical, could there be a birthplace for Rama.

Is Rama historical? Also is Ayodhya of today that birthplace of Rama?

This is a vast topic by itself, deserving a separate discussion, in a much broader light. Hence, we have kept Ayodhya and its history, out of the purview of this book and have discussed it using a wholistic approach, in our separate title, **"Ayodhya – War and Peace".**

In the last decade or so, the scientific advancements that have taken place, have helped scientific historians, revisit the text for historical proofs.

Literature and local legends have continued to keep alive the image of Rama as a popular legendary hero, a righteous man, a noble King, a God.

The historicity of Rama manifests with the ability to date Rama and the *Rama Setu,* to around 5100 BCE, i.e., 7100 years ago, and the conviction of the same grows with an integrated wholistic approach that combines traditional data and scientific validations along with a new technique of dating, Archaeo-Astronomy.

This approach integrates scientific corroborating evidences in the form of,

- Astronomical Sky charts using modern scientific tools
- Geological surveys and research
- Archaeological excavations

- Authentic travelogues of the foreign visitors to India
- Published Government Gazettes
- Historical records and notes from the archives of other countries, such as British Records
- Recent research works of many scientists and other individuals

with the information inherent in our culture such as,

- data available with the traditional scholar community
- native knowledge of the locals
- geography and topology of the land
- local legends and traditions

This wholistic compilation, is the result of careful scrutiny and validation of the information from the above listed various sources and then collation of the same in an integrated, interdisciplinary manner, which it rightfully deserves.

Acknowledgements

We have been singularly fortunate to have been born in this land of ancient wisdom and seers. We owe a lot to our parents who have brought us into this world and provided for us the right education, upbringing and guidance. The values and tradition of this ancient culture and civilization inculcated in us by our family and teachers is what has formed the basis for our work at Bharath Gyan. We owe a lot to our family and friends for their continued support and encouragement in our endeavour.

Having embarked on our quest, many scholars, thinkers and students of the knowledge of India have come forward and helped us in this collation. Some have helped by offering data and some through their questions that made us think and look for the data.

Many traditional scholars have patiently tolerated our inquisitiveness and have laboriously searched and retrieved from the ancient texts, the data we had requested of them and explained the same to us in simple layman terms. Without their mastery over old and new, their knowledge, their mind-set and support, this bridge from the ancient to the present day, would never have been built.

When faced with the task of dissemination, many friends, experts, patrons and guides have come forward to help review our works and take it to stages of production and distribution. We owe a lot to their support without which, this compilation could not have seen the light of the day.

More specifically, we would like to thank His Holiness Sri Sri Ravishankar, for the faith reposed in us and our work and for offering us a platform, to share the knowledgebase we have collated, with the community at large.

We would be failing in our character, if we do not acknowledge more importantly, the unseen forces which have connected us up with these right sources of information and noble people just in time, just as we were looking for the information and help.

The list is very long and words fail us to thank all sufficiently. Hence we take refuge in the all encompassing words of the 18th century Indian Poet Saint Thyagaraja –

Entharo Mahanu Bhavulu Anthariki Vanadanamulu

There are many noble persons (behind this work) and we salute them all.

Ramayana, The Story Of Rama

India has had many glorious dynasties through the ages. In ancient India, there was once a great dynasty known as the *Surya Vamsa,* solar dynasty. This dynasty had many great kings who apart from waging wars and expanding their territories, carried out many noble deeds for the welfare of their people and their times.

Their noble deeds are etched in the form of legendary stories through the land.

An iconographic representation of Rama

In this noble lineage of *Surya Vamsa,* the greatest of the kings was Rama, the son of King Dasaratha.

The nobility of Rama and the events of His life that brought forth His nobilities has been eulogized in the form of the epic poem Ramayana, by the poet Valmiki, one of the earliest poets of the land, who was also a contemporary of Rama.

Rama was born to King Dasaratha and his first wife Queen Kausalya, in the city of Ayodhya, the capital of the Kosala kingdom, which lay between the north of the Ganga river and south of the Himalayas, on the banks of the

Sarayu river, a tributary of the Ganga. Today this region is in the eastern part of Uttar Pradesh state.

Rama had 3 other brothers born to the 2 other wives of King Dasaratha; Bharatha born to Queen Kaikeyi and twins, Lakshmana and Shatrughana born to Queen Sumitra.

All the brothers grew up learning the art of good administration and righteousness, along with learning how to wield weapons and fight a war.

When Rama was a young prince, Rishi Vishwamitra, sought permission from King Dasaratha to take Rama and Lakshmana along with him, to the forest, to fight the *Rakshasa* who were proving to be a menace in the forests. Post a successful battle with the *Rakshasa,* Vishwamitra took Rama and Lakshamana to the kingdom of Mithila where Rama won the hand of beautiful Sita, the daughter of King Janaka of Mithila, in marriage, after emerging a victor in a contest of lifting and stringing a heavy bow.

Rama breaking bow

After their wedding, Rama and Sita lived in the palace of Dasaratha in Ayodhya, for 12 happy years.

As the legend goes King Dasaratha then decides to anoint Rama as the crown prince. On this occasion of the pre coronation of Rama as crown prince, Dasaratha's second Queen, Kaikeyi, asks Dasaratha to exercise the 2 boons awarded to her, earlier by King Dasaratha.

As one of the boons, she asks for her son Prince Bharatha to be appointed as the crown prince instead of Rama and as the second boon, she asks for Rama to be sent on a 14 year exile to the forest.

Rama leaving for exile

In adherence to the wishes of his parents, Rama along with his wife Sita and accompanied by his other brother Lakshmana leaves for the forest, to live in exile for the next 14 years.

King Dasaratha unable to bear the separation of his dearest son Rama, breathes his last soon after.

Prince Bharatha, who was not present in Ayodhya during all these events returns from his maternal grandfather's house in Kekeya. On learning about the events that had transpired and out of love and veneration for his brother Rama, Bharatha refuses to become the King of Ayodhya and insists on waiting the 14 year period as a caretaker only.

Rama, Sita and Lakshmana undergo many a travails in the forest during their exile. They also meet and befriend many sages and tribals during their exile. In their last year of exile, Surpanaka, the sister of Ravana, the King of Lanka, happens to sight Rama in His forest dwelling in Panchavati, present day Nasik, in the Western state of Maharashtra and is smitten by His handsome looks.

She proposes to Rama, but He declines. She then proposes to Lakshmana, who also declines. Out of jealousy, Surpanaka then rushes towards Sita to eliminate Her. Lakshmana springs forth to the defence of Sita and cuts Surpanaka's nose. The injured and insulted Surpanaka rushes to her brothers Khar and Dushan in the nearby forest and instigates them to avenge her insult by attacking Rama and Lakshmana. In the battle that ensues between Khar and Dushan with Rama and Lakshmana, Khar and Dushan are killed.

Surpanaka imploring with Ravana after Nose Cut

Surpanaka, then rushes to her other brother, Ravana, the King of Lanka and narrates the episode of her nose cut and pleads with him to avenge her insult.

Ravana along with his uncle Mareecha comes to the Dandakaranya forest where Rama is camping along with Sita and Lakshmana. Mareecha takes the form of a golden deer and entices Sita who sends Rama and Lakshmana to bring Her the deer. In their absence, Ravana, in the guise of a hermit, kidnaps Sita and takes Her away to Lanka in his aircraft, the *Pushpaka Vimana.*

Ravana disguised as a hermit to kidnap Sita

Enroute, Sita drops Her jewellery which come into the hands of the *Vanara* living on the hills in Kishkinda. Kishkinda is the present day Hampi, in the southern state of Karnataka in India. Rama and Lakshmana in their search for Sita, encounter Hanuman one of the *Vanara* and he takes them to their leader, the ousted *Vanara* Prince Sugreeva.

Sugreeva offers to help Rama, provided Rama can help kill his brother, Vali, the strong *Vanara* King, who had not only thrown Sugreeva out of the kingdom but had also appropriated Sugreeva's wife much against her wishes. Rama kills Vali and places Sugreeva on the throne of Kishkinda.

Rama & Lakshmana with Sugreeva and other *Vanara*

Sugreeva then deputes his *Vanara* soldiers in all directions to search for Sita.

Hanuman, one of the strongest *Vanara,* is part of the search party which goes south. He leaps across the sea and enters the kingdom of Lanka.

Hanuman crossing the seas

There he finds Sita sitting forlorn in a grove, *Ashoka Vatika,* surrounded by the *Rakshasi* of Lanka.

Hanuman finds Sita in *Ashoka Vatika*

After confirming Sita's identity, he identifies himself to Sita and promises to bring Rama soon to wage a war with Ravana and take Her back home.

Sugreeva then prepares his *Vanara* army for marching to Lanka.

They reach the seashore of South India near Rameswaram, build a bridge over the seas and cross over to Lanka.

Vanara building the bridge

In the meanwhile, Vibhishana, one of the younger brothers of Ravana, tries to reason with Ravana and convince him to return Sita back to Rama, as otherwise a lot of harm could befall Lanka and its people, since the deed of kidnapping Sita was an unjust act. Ravana however does not pay heed to Vibhishana and banishes him from the kingdom. Vibhishana, being righteous, joins Rama in the war against Ravana for righteousness.

The fight between Rama and Ravana

Once on the shores of Lanka, the *Vanara* army fight with the *Rakshasa* army of Ravana. In this war, Ravana loses his other brother Kumbakarna as well as many of his trusted aides. Ravana's son Meghanada or Indrajit as he was popularly called, puts up a valiant battle and renders Lakshmana unconscious. Hanuman at the behest of the physician Sushena, brings the Sanjeevani herb from the Himalayas to revive Lakshmana.

Subsequently Meghanada is also killed in the battle.

The fierce battle then continues between Rama and Ravana, in which Ravana finally succumbs to the arrows of Rama.

The victorious Rama, then arranges for Vibhishana to be crowned the king of Lanka and leaves for Ayodhya with Sita and Lakshmana in Ravana's aircraft, *Pushpaka Vimana,* loaned to them by Vibhishana.

Rama, Sita and Lakshmana returning in *Pushpaka Vimana*

On reaching Ayodhya, Rama was crowned the king of Ayodhya and He ruled over the kingdom wisely in a just and prosperous manner for many years. Hanuman stayed behind with Rama as His devoted aide and the coronation of Rama depicted in many art forms, has continued to remind us of Rama and His noble ways.

Rama's *Pattabhishekam* - Coronation

As the legend continues, Sita delivered twin sons – Luva and Kusha who learnt the Ramayana from Valmiki and narrated it to Rama.

It is through them that the epic poem of Ramayana by Valmiki and the legend of Rama, came to be known popularly and continued to be passed on from generation to generation as the history or *Itihasa* of the land.

Luva and Kusha narrating Ramayana to Rama

In the light of many, including Indians and Sri Lankans, confused over whether Ramayana is a myth or a real life history of their lands with real life people, a detail examination of the events, data and facts from the text converging with local topology, language, customs and belief of the people across times lends credibility to the story as history.

Ramayana, An *Itihasa*

WHAT IS AN *ITIHASA*?

What is *itihasa* and why is Ramayana called an *itihasa?*

The word *itihasa* may be split as *iti+ha+asa,* meaning, "it thus happened".

Out of all the ancient Indian literature, including the *Veda,* the *Purana,* the *Shastra, Kavya* and many such others, there are only 2 works which are termed as *itihasa,* they being Valmiki's Ramayana and Vyasa's Mahabharatha.

Valmiki composing Ramayana

Vyasa dictating Mahabharatha

Valmiki's Ramayana is a work that narrates the story of the life of Rama, who was one of the noblest of men and a righteous king of the kingdom of Ayodhya, in ancient India. It is a biography that showcases and highlights the attributes of the noblest king of Valmiki's times and of all times.

Vyasa's Mahabharatha is a work that covers the history of the Hastinapura Kingdom and its dynasty including the great Kurukshetra war that was fought within the clan, for righteousness and the kingdom. Mahabharatha also covers in parallel some of the incidents in the life time of Krishna, who established the kingdom city of Dwaraka and played a key role as an arbitrator in the events leading to the Kurukshetra war.

Both Rama and Krishna have been revered, over thousands of years, by millions of Indians in India and the world over, as divinities and are considered to be incarnations of Lord Vishnu on earth. But that does not take away the historicity of these personages as the millions of Indians have also strongly believed in the historicity of these personages and their times.

These 2 *itihasa* along with continuing local legends and traditions across thousands of years have kept alive the descriptions, the memories of those times, people and places and have been providing the grounds for this strong belief in the historicity of this land and these personages.

While one of the roles of these *itihasa* is to act as a chronicle of the events, these *itihasa* also had a more encompassing role to play in documenting history. Instead of documenting the events and dates as disjoint records, they were written as a story with great details to also serve as a guidebook for people to learn a lesson or two from history and conduct their present lives suitably – the real role that history is supposed to serve.

VALMIKI RAMAYANA – A HISTORICAL BIOGRAPHY

Valmiki Ramayana is a historical biography because Valmiki, the author of the original Ramayana text was a contemporary of Rama. This has been explicitly stated in the text itself. This story was not penned a few hundred years after the life of Rama. In fact, Valmiki was the guardian to the wife and sons of Rama.

Valmiki, author of Ramayana with Luva and Kusha, the sons of Rama

This one fact gives it the credibility of being an authentic historical account. If you look at various historical texts world over, we find that the records of the events which happened, have usually been written down as history, about a few hundred or even few thousand years post the events having taken place, leaving room for some gaps.

In the case of Valmiki Ramayana, it is a text written by a person, Valmiki, who was a contemporary to the people and period of event. Valmiki also plays an integral role in the events of Ramayana.

As to the authenticity of the content of Valmiki Ramayana that he had collated, Valmiki himself vouches for it, when he meets Rama for the first time and introduces himself as:

Prachetsoahem dasmey putroh raghavnandany

Ne ismarahmeanritam vakyamimo tu tav putroko ||

- Valmiki Ramayana 7.96.19

i.e., Valmiki proudly says to Rama,

"I am the 10th son of Pracheta, and I

never remember speaking even one untrue sentence."

This emphatic statement of Valmiki gives a strong dimension of credibility to his Ramayana.

That the Ramayana is an *itihasa* and that it was written by Valmiki during the lifetime of Rama, His wife Sita, and their sons Lava and Kusha can been seen from the language in the text. Ramayana is not written in the past tense or future tense, it is primarily written in the present tense. This goes to indicate to us from a different angle, that it is a biography by Valmiki of the happenings during his times.

The focus of Valmiki in his Ramayana, was to showcase the noble qualities of Rama. To bring out these qualities better and to aid our understanding of the same, in the right context, Valmiki also included the history of Rama and His times in his work.

RAMAYANA – A STORY ON RIGHTEOUSNESS

What prompted Valmiki to write the Ramayana *Itihasa?*

Much before Valmiki had come to know of Rama, his quest for a righteous person and his introduction to Rama as a result, is explained allegorically, as his meeting with the divine wanderer Narada, to whom he poses a question –

"Who is the greatest man who ever lived?"

Valmiki and Narada interaction
Starting Point
for the Epic - Ramayana

Narada then narrates the story of Rama, King of Ayodhya, in a few terse, factual lines.

The inquisitiveness of Valmiki is kindled and he then goes about compiling information on this noble person, from the people who have interacted with Rama. Then, armed with all that data, he elaborates the story in poetry, scripting Ramayana. It is later in the unfolding of the story, that Valmiki himself gives shelter to Sita and to Her to be born twins and the authenticity of the story gets validated thereby. Later in the story the two sons of Rama, narrate the story of Ramayana, as taught to them by Valmiki, to their father Rama, when they see Him in the palace for the first time, thus validating the authenticity of text, with Rama Himself.

What is to be noted here is that, Valmiki did not intend the Ramayana epic to be a historical story, but an account of the noblest person of all. To bring out and express the noble characteristics of Rama, Valmiki used the chronicle of events in Rama's life, as the canvas to bring out these qualities of Rama.

In the bargain, we, so many thousands of years later, are therefore able to find data, that gives us an insight into the dates, history and period of Rama's times.

OTHER RAMAYANA VERSIONS

Ramayana being a popular story of India, many authors down the timeline have also written their own versions of Ramayana.

Kalidasa - Raghuvamsa

Kalidasa, the great Samskrt poet of the 5th century CE wrote *Raghuvamsa*, his poetry on Rama.

Kamban - Kamba Ramayana

The Tamil poet Kamban wrote his version of Ramayana called *Kamba Ramayana*, over 1000 years ago.

Goswami Tulsidas - Ram Charitra Manas

Goswami Tulasidas wrote *Ram Charitra Manas* in the 17th century CE.

These 3 and such other eminent authors across India have penned the story eulogizing the Indian hero and attributing divinity to Rama.

These later day texts cannot be termed as being completely historical, because they are based on the information available at their times.

Hence these later versions are not called *Itihasa*. They are popularly known as *kavya* or beautiful poetry.

In contrast to all this, the Ramayana written by Valmiki alone can be considered as authentic historical text, which is why the text has been classified as *Itihasa,* meaning 'it thus happened'.

The *Puranic* text of India also mention the details on the story of Rama. The stories mentioned in the *Puranic* texts and the original Ramayana of Valmiki corroborate each other in many a places. This adds further credibility to the Valmiki Ramayana text being rightly termed as *Itihasa* – it thus happened – a historical text.

If there is so much history in India, then how did the Indian Texts get termed as "Mythology"?

FROM HISTORY TO MYTHOLOGY

When the British started ruling India, they were disturbed by the high ethos of the Indians which did not lend itself conducive, for the British, to rule over India. Not only that, they were even more disturbed by the influence, the Indian knowledge systems and practices, were having on the English officers deputed to India, who according to them were becoming more *"Brahminised"* and had started advocating the cause and systems of India.

The classic example of this influence was Warren Hastings, the Governor General of the East India Company. Warren Hastings played a major role in capturing much of India for the East India Company. His contemporary, Col. Alexander Walker, describes Hastings as, *"wicked, mischievous and disingenuous"*, and in his opinion, *"it was impossible to pardon his tergiversations."*

This Warren Hastings, during his Governorship in India, met a lot of local scholars and learnt a lot about Indian culture and started adapting the Indian ethos during his tenure here. This change of his was termed as *"Brahminisation of the Englishmen"*, by the board of the Directors of the East India Company, who realized that something must be done if the British were to control and increase their stranglehold on India. Towards this effect, the Board of Directors of the East India Company, organized a debate in England between 1806 and 1808 on the high morality of Hindus among officers who came back from India.

30 papers, of over 100 pages each were presented during these debates.

To get a control on this situation, it was then strategised by the British, that the best way to rule over the Indians and also curb India's mental and spiritual influence on the Englishmen, would be to demean India's culture, history and knowledge. To this end, the native history books would have to carry such information that would create self doubt amongst Indians, about themselves. This mindset, would help the British overlord over the Indians, better.

THE HISTORY OF INDIA – BY THE BRITISH

To achieve this objective, the British then appointed 2 persons to write the History of India, without visiting India, lest they get influenced by its rich culture.

In 1813, Mr. James Mill and Mr. Charles Grant, wrote the **"History of India",** wherein they classified most of the literature of India as Mythological.

This History book formed the syllabus for the English administrators who had to pass through Helebary College England, before being deputed to India, so that their impressions of India would already be influenced and prejudiced, even before they stepped on Indian soil.

This book also found its way into the educational institutions of India to complete the other task of disorienting the Indian minds.

Helebary College

James Mill

Charles Grant

A CASE OF FLAWED ASSUMPTIONS

Mill and Grant classified Indian texts as Mythological on the following 4 grounds:

1. The events in these texts seemed to go before the date of creation of the earth fixed by Reverend James Ussher, the Archbishop of Ireland, as 23rd October, 4004 BC, 9 AM. Hence these texts which describe India and the existence of its civilization prior to this time, could not be real and must be mythical or imaginary.

   The fact that this world was not created on 23rd October, 4004 BC, has now been proven wrong by modern cosmology and traditional archaeological finds. Hence this premise of Mill and Grant has been found to be flawed.

2. It was held by the colonial British, that Alexander defeated Porus in 326 BCE and spread culture and civilized thought to India. Until then Indians were uncivilized barbarians. So the civilization described in these texts which seemed to be more advanced in science, technology, culture, philosophy and linguistics could not have existed prior to the arrival of Alexander and hence the texts must be mythical.

   Not only has the existence of a civilized India, prior to the arrival of Alexander, been proved right, beyond an iota of doubt, the talk of the defeat of Porus in the hands of Alexander, is also now being questioned, with the uncovering of various pre biblical texts and with the piecing together of various circumstantial evidences which point to the contrary, namely, Alexander being wounded and defeated by Porus. The findings of our integrated research at Bharath Gyan, on this topic of Alexander vs Porus, which we shall bring out soon in our series, also confirms that Porus defeated Alexander. Hence this premise of Mill and Grant is also flawed.

3. The British had already come up with the concept of the Aryan Invasion of India, according to which, it was the Aryans who spread culture and civilized thought to India and that until then Indians were uncivilized barbarians. Hence, again, the description in the traditional texts of India, which described a civilization that seemed to be more advanced in science, technology, culture, philosophy and linguistics and seemed to have existed prior to the Aryan Invasion, clashed with the Aryan Invasion theory. Hence they had to classify these texts as mythical.

   The Aryan Invasion Theory has now been dismissed by the Western historians themselves, as a figment of concoction by the British, to justify their occupation of India. By painting some of the Indians themselves as their brethren, belonging to the Aryan race, who had invaded and settled in India by defeating the original inhabitants, the Dravidians, and called them as lower castes, the British wanted to establish themselves as a rightful occupier of this Indian territory and beneficiary of its natural resources.

   This Aryan – Dravidian classification has now been proven to be racially incorrect, as the entire Indian population has been found to belong to the same race, despite their differences in features and complexion. Also the study of traditional Indian text has thrown to light, how the terminologies Aryan and Dravidian, were based on geographical division and not racial, cultural or civilizational differences. Thus this premise of Mill and Grant also is found to be flawed.

4. Mill and Grant had held that, the genealogies in the *Purana* were incoherent and hence the *Puranic* and other texts were imaginary or mythical.

It is to be noted that while the *Puranic* texts of India, contained genealogies, their focus was to showcase key human achievements in the light of *Dharma,* the principles to be followed, basically lessons for life. Given this, there is a therefore a good possibility for gaps or inconsistencies while discussing the order in genealogy, but that cannot detract from the historicity of the texts.

A HUGE PRICE TO PAY BY INDIA

Thus, on all these 4 grounds, Mill and Grant's assumptions, for classifying the Indian literature as mythological, have been found flawed. But alas, their work left such an impression on the minds of Indians, that the confusion created in the minds of Indians lasts to this day and Indians doubt the authenticity of their own knowledge, literature and history.

In the light of these assumptions being flawed, these texts need to be restored to their original classification as *Itihasa,* historical texts; the classification, that they enjoyed prior to this incorrect reclassification as mythology. That would bring in a new dimension to our understanding of world history and civilizations.

Let us examine what the word "mythology" means.

WHAT IS MYTHOLOGY?

The word mythology or myth shares its etymological roots with the Indian Samskrt word *'mithia'* which in Samskrt means *'untrue'*. Any text that has been termed as mythological by classification means that, *"the contents mentioned therein are untrue or figments of imagination"*.

WHAT QUALIFIES AS HISTORY?

What are the parameters, that can guide us in evaluating a text as a record of history?

When an established textual description of an event, is corroborated with:

- the geography of the land
- the archaeological evidences if any, tally with the descriptions
- there are repeated historical references through the land for the events
- the genealogy of the characters of the text can be traced through the times
- a date can be attributed to the events in history using scientific methods, then the text becomes an authentic narration of history.

Having laid down the parameters, we shall examine going forward, whether Ramayana is indeed a historical text of this land and whether Rama was really a historic person and if so when could all these events have happened?

THE NEED FOR AN INTERDISCIPLINARY APPROACH

The parameters for concluding if an event is part of history or not, emphasize the need for examining it from various angles. It calls for an interdisciplinary approach to check for corroborations of the event, from across different fields.

Much to the consternation of many post British historians, who continue to adopt an outdated, colonial stand on the antiquity as well as roots of India and her culture, it is to be noted that there are very few civilizations that are as ancient and continuous as India.

Hence the branches of history and archaeology as practiced today, need to take a relook, at the techniques of tracing the history of such civilizations. A limited and compartmentalized view could lead to findings that go contrary to tradition and practices of the land that have actually survived across millennia.

In the case of tracing the historicity of Rama, the interdisciplinary approach followed here, takes into account data and facts from the following fields;

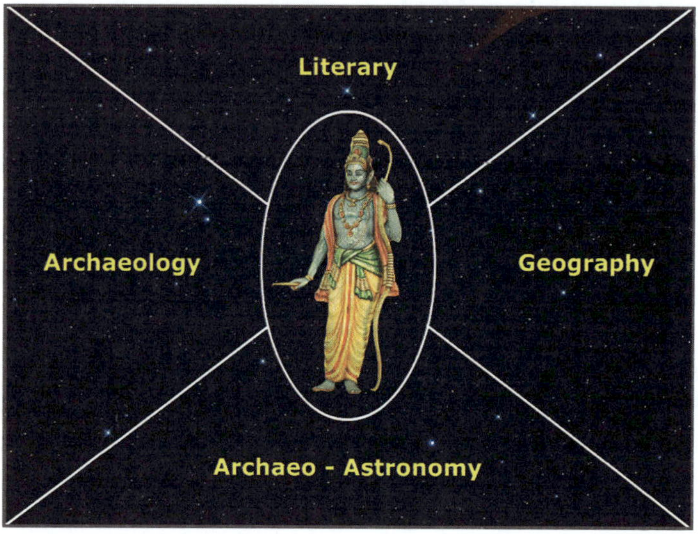

1. Literature
2. Geography
3. Archaeology – both Traditional archaeology on land and Marine Archaeology for studying undersea structures
4. Archaeo – Astronomy

From The Field Of Literature

THE FAMILY TREE OF RAMA

The lineage of Rama, both before and after Him, has been extensively documented, not only in the Ramayana but also in the other texts, such as the Mahabaratha and the Bhagavatha Purana. The Bhagavatha Purana is one of the 18 *Purana,* which among other things also speaks about the genealogy of various dynasties.

The extensive family tree chart that follows, gives us the list of kings in the *Surya Vamsa,* Solar dynasty, lineage to which Rama belongs.

This lineage starts from Kashyapa and his wife Aditi. Kashyapa is regarded as the father figure of those times, after whom comes the famous king Ikshwaku. From, Ikshvaku, dynasty from which Rama hailed.

There have been many prominent kings in this glorious dynasty. Some of the popular ones among them, have been boxed here for our easy notice.

In one of our future works titled **"Ganga – Bhagiratha Prayathna",** we shall be looking at the extraordinary efforts of the kings from King Sagara to King Bhagiratha, in bringing us the Ganga river.

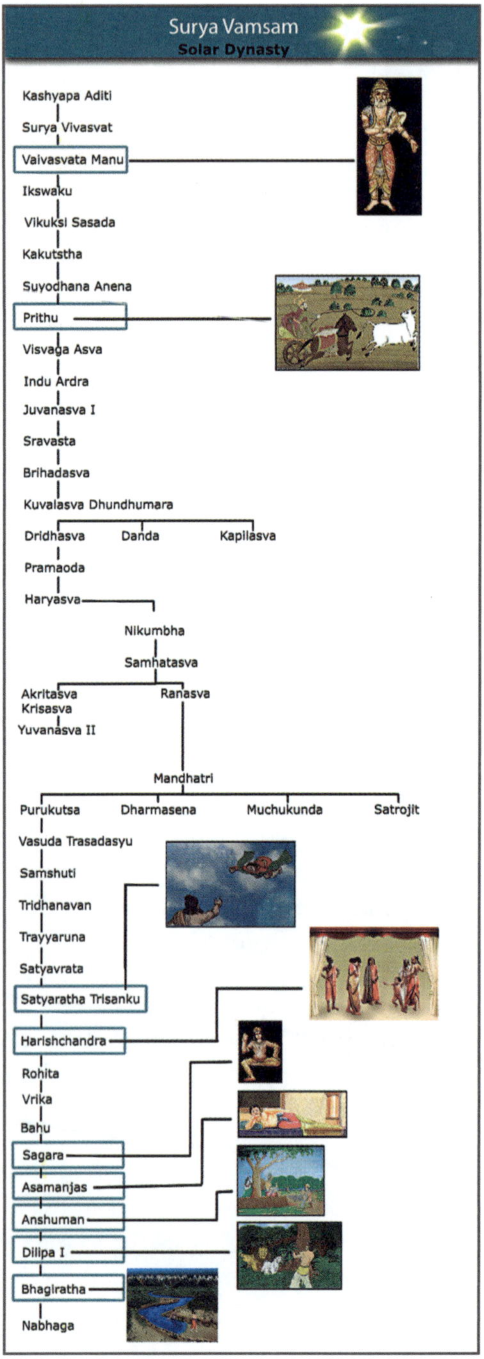
Surya Vamsam
Solar Dynasty
Kashyapa Aditi
Surya Vivasvat
Vaivasvata Manu
Ikswaku
Vikuksi Sasada
Kakutstha
Suyodhana Anena
Prithu
Visvaga Asva
Indu Ardra
Juvanasva I
Sravasta
Brihadasva
Kuvalasva Dhundhumara
Dridhasva
Danda
Kapilasva
Pramaoda
Haryasva
Nikumbha
Samhatasva
Akritasva
Krisasva
Yuvanasva II
Ranasva
Mandhatri
Purukutsa
Dharmasena
Muchukunda
Satrojit
Vasuda Trasadasyu
Samshuti
Tridhanavan
Trayyaruna
Satyavrata
Satyaratha Trisanku
Harishchandra
Rohita
Vrika
Bahu
Sagara
Asamanjas
Anshuman
Dilipa I
Bhagiratha
Nabhaga

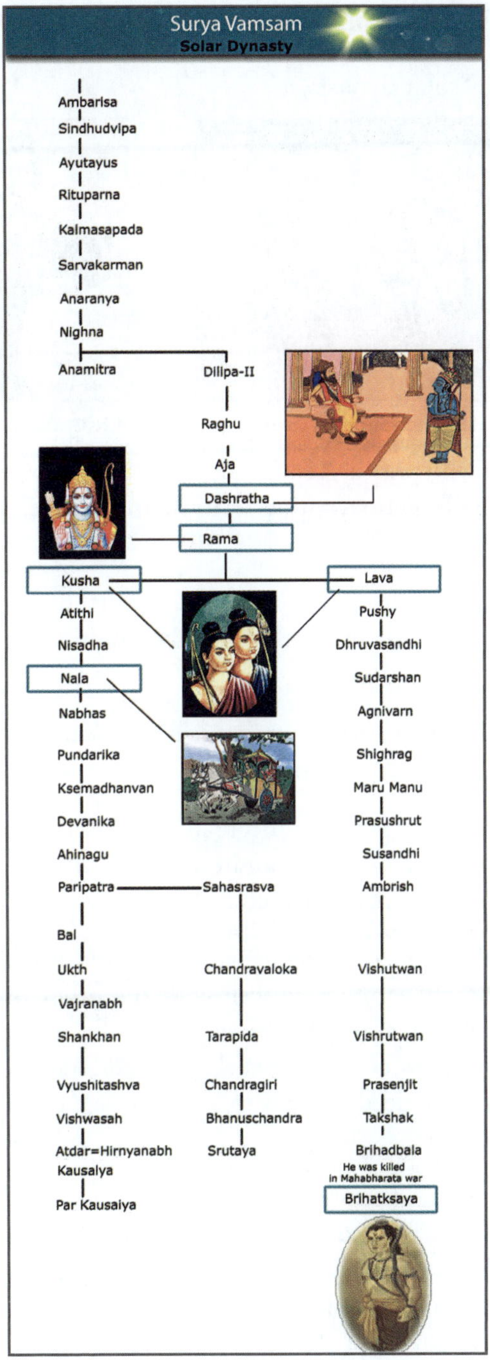
Surya Vamsam
Solar Dynasty
Ambarisa
Sindhudvipa
Ayutayus
Rituparna
Kalmasapada
Sarvakarman
Anaranya
Nighna
Anamitra
Dilipa-II
Raghu
Aja
Dashratha
Rama
Kusha
Lava
Atithi
Nisadha
Nala
Nabhas
Pundarika
Ksemadhanvan
Devanika
Ahinagu
Paripatra
Bal
Ukth
Vajranabh
Shankhan
Vyushitashva
Vishwasah
Atdar=Hirnyanabh
Kausalya
Par Kausalya
Sahasrasva
Chandravaloka
Tarapida
Chandragiri
Bhanuschandra
Srutaya
Pushy
Dhruvasandhi
Sudarshan
Agnivarn
Shighrag
Maru Manu
Prasushrut
Susandhi
Ambrish
Vishutwan
Vishrutwan
Prasenjit
Takshak
Brihadbala
He was killed in Mahabharata war
Brihatksaya

Harishchandra, the king known for his honesty, whose story moved and moulded the views of Mohandas Karamchand Gandhi, also belonged to this solar dynasty.

Raja Harishchandra - Drama

M.K.Gandhi as a child

Nala, the king who was a great cook and also an expert horse rider, along with his wife Damayanti, is a household name. He came from this dynasty.

Raghu was another illustrious king of this very dynasty. Rama and successors of Rama are referred to as belonging to *Raghu kula* or dynasty of Raghu.

The question that may arise in one's mind is – *"Is it not possible to create such a family tree for even a fictional person?"*

While it is definitely possible to create a fictional family tree for a fictional person, it will not corroborate with the other texts of the land, as they are only fictional in character.

In the case of Ramayana, the sequence, events and deeds of the various kings in the lineage, corroborate well with the other texts of the land and more importantly also with the sequence of their occurrence. This consistency across texts, across events, across times, across geography gives credibility, that, it is indeed a family tree of a lineage that is historical.

We can see that this family tree does not stop with Rama, but goes on to 30 generations and more after Rama. Infact, well down in this lineage from Rama, one of the kings, Brihadbala takes part in the Kurukshetra War of the Mahabharatha period (around 3100 BCE). Brihadbala fights on the side of Duryodhana the *Kaurava* prince, the antagonist, against the *Pandava* brothers, the protagonists, and is killed by Abhimanyu, the son of Arjuna the *Pandava* and the nephew of Krishna, in the infamous battle of the *Chakravyuha.*

Abhimanyu
An Illustration from
Amar Chitra Katha

Many other texts also refer to the lineage of Rama. The extensive corroborative nature between and within these texts, clearly vindicates the historical nature of this family tree.

Apart from references in the various *Purana,* there is specific reference to the personages of the lineage and their kingdoms, in the *Veda* too.

- Ikshvaku – the head of the lineage is mentioned in the *Rig Veda* verse 10.60.4.4.
- The Town plan of Ayodhya with 9 Gates is mentioned in *Atharva Veda,* verse 18.3.16.
- The *Rishi,* sages, Vishwamitra, Vasishta and Bharadwaja, who figure in the events of the Ramayana period and life of Rama, also find mention in the *Rig Veda.*

A PERSIAN'S CHRONICLE

Mahmud of Ghazini

Al-Biruni

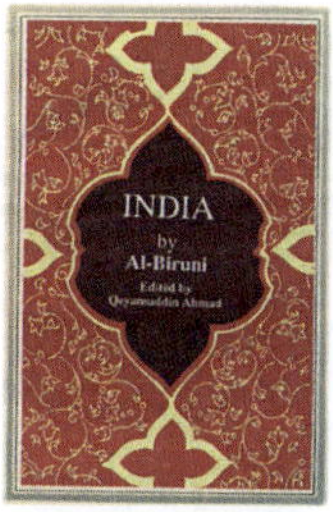

Kitabul Hind

Al-Biruni, was a Persian Chronicler who came to India in 1030 CE along with Mahmud of Ghazini. While Mahmud of Ghazini plundered India, Al-Biruni took great pains in chronicling the sciences, the history and the overall knowledge of India. This chronicle is known as *"Kitabul Hind".*

In this book, in more than a few places, Al-Biruni mentions Rama as a historical person, some of the relevant quotes being:

"The eastern mountain chain, extends towards the east, then turns towards the south, until it reaches the great ocean, where parts of it penetrate into the sea, at the place called Dike of Rama."

Dike of Rama

Dike here referring to the bridge built by Rama, between India and Sri Lanka, known today as Adam's bridge.

Describing further, he says it is *"Opposite Sarandib, the distance of the sea between them is 12 farsakh. Between Ramsher and Setubandha 2 farsakh. Setubandha means bridge of the ocean. It is the Dike of Rama, the son of Dasaratha, which he built from the continent to the castle Lanka. At present it consists of isolated mountains between which the ocean flows."*

- Kitabu'l Hind, Page 122

This observation of Al-Biruni over 1000 years ago, speaks of Rama purely from a historical perspective and also of the bridge that was built to Lanka across the seas in the south eastern tip of India.

INDIAN PERSIAN TEXTS

There a few Persian texts of India, which look at Rama and Ramayana, purely from a historical perspective.

The prominent among them are the Mughal period texts written by some of the prominent Mughal rulers of India.

Begum Hamida Banu

Begum Hamida Banu was the daughter in law of the 1st Mughal King of India, Babar.

Humayun

Mughal King Babar

Begum Hamida Banu, was the wife of Mughal Emperor Humayun.

Begum Hamida Banu, was a woman of great qualities. She commissioned a pictorial Ramayana, as she related to the story and also considered it as a historical text of her land.

Here are a few incidents that highlight some of her great qualities and also why and how she related to the story of Ramayana.

Hamida Banu's marriage to Humayun Akbarnama

Courtesy : Cynthia Hazar Polsky Collection, USA

Emperor Humayun had a dream, which was explained to him by Shayak Ahmed Jami, that, if he married the young Hamida Banu, the son born to them would be the king of the land. So he had called for Hamida Banu, a few times.

Hamida Banu, went to see him and offer her respects.

When she was called for a second time, she is known to have replied *"If it is to pay my respects, I was exalted by paying my respects the other day; why should I come again? To see the king once is lawful; a second time it is forbidden. I shall not come."*

This shows that she was "a woman of substance."

Later, when she did marry Humayun, she was constantly on the run with Humayun, fleeing from Sher Shah Suri and the 2 brothers of Humayun, Kamran and Aksari who were chasing them. In this, she related to and sympathized with Sita, who in the forest, moved from one place to another along with Her husband, who was in exile.

While Sita was in exile for 14 years, Hamida Banu was on the run for 12 years.

As her future born son was prophesied to become the king of the land, she also related her state with that of Kausalya, the mother of Rama.

All these factors combined, made her commission a pictorial Ramayana.

Some of these paintings are now housed in different museums across the globe.

Dasaratha's *Yagna* for an offspring

Courtesy : Museum Reitberg, Zurich

Rishi Vishwamitra taking Rama & Lakshmana to the forest to fight the *Rakshasa*

Courtesy : Museum Reitberg, Zurich

The Slaying of Surpanaka

Courtesy : Museum Reitberg, Zurich

Rama, Sita & Lakshmana taking leave of King Dasaratha, before leaving for the forest

Courtesy: Nour Foundation, London

Akbar

Akbar

Hamida Banu's son Akbar, who went on to become one of the most prominent Emperors of India, also had a Ramayana commissioned in the Persian language.

Dasaratha's *Putresti Yagna*

Courtesy:Maharaja Sawai Man Singh II Museum, Jaipur

Exile of Sita

Courtesy : Maharaja Sawai Man Singh II Museum, Jaipur

Abdur Rahim Khan-e-khan

Abdur Rahim Khan-e-khan was a courtier in the court of Akbar. He had also commissioned a pictorial Ramayana. In his version of the Ramayana, every chapter ends with the phrase *"Khan e khanan"*.

Dasaratha's *Putresti Yagna*
From Ramayana commissioned by
Abdur Rahim Khan-e-Khan

Courtesy:
Freer Gallery of Art, Smithsonian Institute,
Washington DC

Aligarh Muslim University

Apart from the above, Aligarh Muslim University in India too has a Valmiki Ramayana in the Persian language.

Valmiki Ramayana of Aligarh Muslim University

Aligarh Muslim University

There are these many Persian editions and version of Ramayana by the Mughals in India, because they all considered Rama as a historical King of their land and were exemplifying Rama's historical nature and noble qualities.

Pakistani Poet

It was not only the medieval Persian writers, who considered Rama as a historical person, even the present day poet of the Persian and Urdu language, Professor. Allama Mohammed Iqbal, the renowned poet of Pakistan, in his eulogy, describes Rama as India's *Imam-e-Hind*, meaning, **"Noblest of Indians".**

Professor Allama Muhammad Iqbal

خودي کا
خودي کا سر نہاں لا الہ الا اللہ
خودي ہے تيغ فساں لا الہ لا اللہ

یہ دور اپنے ابراہیم کي تلاش میں ہے
صنم کدہ ہے جہاں، لا الہ لا اللہ

کیا ہے تو نے متاع غرور کا سوادا
فریب سود و زیاں ، لا الہ لا اللہ

یہ مال و دولت دنیا، یہ رشتہ و پیوند
بتان وہم و گماں، لا الہ لا اللہ

یہ نغمہ فسل گل و لالا کا نہیں پابند
بہار ہو کہ خزاں، لا الہ لا اللہ
اگر چہ بت ہیں جماعت کي آستینوں میں
مجھے ہے حکم اذاں،لا الہ لا اللہ

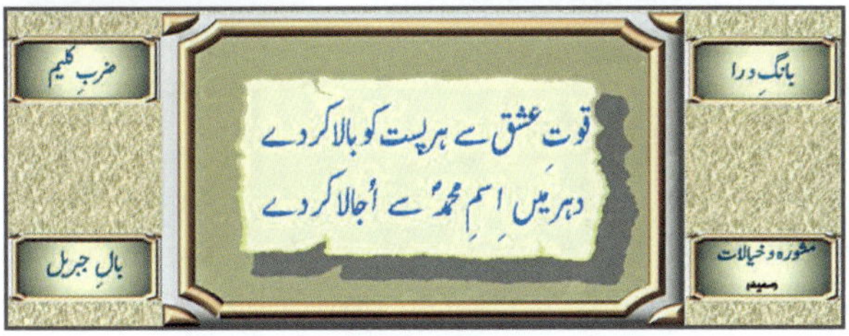

The Persian Eulogy by Prof. Iqbal

THE TAMIL *SANGAM* TEXT

In Tamil literature, there is a period known as *Sangam* age, a prehistoric period.

The literature of this period is known as *Sangam* age literature.

Some of the famous texts of this period are *Agananuru, Purananuru* and *Silapathikaram.*

These texts are considered to be secular in nature.

In these three texts, Rama is mentioned as a part of the conversation, from a historical perspective.

This goes to tell us that the events of Ramayana are much earlier to the *Sangam* period and the deeds of Rama were well known to the local Tamil people. Rama was popular enough to be used as an example, without giving any explanatory prefixes.

Let us see some of these references to Rama in the *Sangam* texts.

Agananuru

முழங்கு இரும் பௌவம் இரங்கும் முன் துறை
வெல்போர் இராமர் அருமறைக்கு அவித்த
பல்வீழ் ஆலம் போல
ஒலி அவிந்தன்று, இவ் அழுங்கல் ஊரே.

***Agananuru* - 70th Song - *Neithal Thinai* - last 4 lines**
Poet: Madurai Thamizh Koothanar Kaduvan Mallanar

These 4 lines quote Rama and an incident around His life, as a simile to explain a situation in the text.

The hero came back and wed the maiden and this quietened the gossip that had started with the news that he was coming to see her.

The gossip of the people living in the town came to a sudden stop, the way, the noisy birds on the big banyan tree by the sea shore suddenly stopped making sound, when Rama, a warrior capable of winning wars, who was sitting under that tree in deep thought and consultation with the Vanara, on the strategy for winning the battle, raised His hand and asked the birds to stop making sound.

Rama's raised hand quietening the noisy birds
- Artist Adriraj Paul

An illustration depicting the hero coming to wed the maiden

Puranaanooru

The Chola King *Elanchet Chenni* presented the poet with many gifts including jewels, for his talent in poetry. The poet distributed the articles to his parents, family members and relatives.

விரல் செறி மரபின செவித் தொடக் குநரும்
செவித் தொடர் மரபின விரற் செறிக்குநரும்
அரைக்கமை மரபின மிடற்று யாக்குநரும்
மிடற்றமை மரபின அரைக்கு யாக்குநரும்

கடுந்தெறல் இராமன் உடன்புணர் சீதையை
வலித்தகை அரக்கன் வெளவிய ஞான்றை
நிலஞ்சேர் மதர் அணி கண்ட குரங்கின்
செம்முகப் பெருங்கிளை இழைப் பொலிந்தாங்கு

***Puranaanooru* 378**
Written by Oon Pathi Pasunkdaiyar

The lines in the poem describe how the people wore the ornaments wrongly. This is compared to how the *Vanara* wrongly wore the ornaments thrown by Sita in Ramayana, while Sita was being carried away by Ravana in his *Vimana*.

Silapathikaram by Ilango Adigal

Silapathikaram is a story of the *Sangam* period set in the court of the *Pandya* King of Madurai. Here the purity of love and justness is brought out through Kannagi, the heroine of the story, whose anger at the unjust treatment meted out to her husband Kovalan by the King, sets fire to the city of Madurai.

Kannagi in *Pandya* court - *Silapathikaram*

Comparing this incident with how the presence of the abducted, chaste Sita in Lanka became the cause for Lanka being set in flames, Ramayana and its events have been referenced many times in this literature.

தாதை ஏவலின் மாதுடன் போகிக்
காதலி நீங்கக் கடுந்துயர் உழந்தோன்
வேத முதல்வோன் பயந்தோன் என்பது
நீ யறிந்திலையோ நெடுமொழியன்றோ

— சிலப்பதிகாரம்
- ஊர்காண் காதை (46-49)

Verse addressed to Kannagi says,

"Your grief cannot be greater than the grief, recounted through the ages, of Rama, who abiding His father's words, went to the forests with His beloved wife, lost Her in the forests and was roaming around in search of Her."

பெருமகன் ஏவல் அல்லது யாங்கணும்
அரசே தஞ்சம் என்று அருங்கான் அடைந்த
அருந்திறல் பிரிந்த அயோத்தி போலப்
பெரும்பெயர் மூதூர் பெரும் பேதுற்றதும்

— சிலப்பதிகாரம்
புறஞ்சேரியிருந்த காதை (63-66)

Kausikan- a Brahmin states,

"Kovalan by your leaving Kaveripoompatinam, it has lost its liveliness. This is similar to Ayodhya bereft of Rama who went to the forest at the behest of His father, the king."

மூவுலகும் ஈரடியான் முறை நிரம்பா வகை முடியத்
தாவியசே வடிசேப்பத் தம்பியொடுங் கான்போந்து
சோ வரணும் போர்மடியத் தொல்இலங்கை கட்டழித்த
சேவகன் சீர் கேளாத செவியென்ன செவியே
திருமால் சீர் கேளாத செவியென்ன செவியே.

— ஆய்ச்சியர் குரவை
- படர்க்கைப் பரவல் (35)

Went to forest with brother. Later destroyed Lanka in a war.

We can see from all these extracts, that the *Sangam* age poets did not eulogise Rama as a divinity, but have referred to Rama as a historical person of their land and as a role model and example, for their then current day situations.

This also shows that Rama was already a popular figure of those days, to be used as a role model.

TAMIL ENCYCLOPAEDIA

Apart from these prehistoric Tamil texts, in the Tamil language encyclopaedia of both, Tamil Nadu in India and of Sri Lanka, the reference to Rama and the bridge construction is only from a historical perspective.

Abithana Chintamani

Abithana Chintamani – Encyclopaedia from India

This encyclopaedia was written in 1899 by A. Singaravelu Mudaliar of India. In page 1628, with reference to Rama and the *Setu* across the seas from India to Sri Lanka, the relevant passage and its translation read as,

சேது — 1. துர்க்கன் பேரன்.

2. (பிர.) பப்ரு குமரன், இவன் குமரன் ஆரத்தன்.

3. இராமமூர்த்தி இராவணனை வதை செய்ய இலங்கைக்குச் செல்கையில் நளன் எனும் வாநரத்தச்சன் வாநரசைந்யங்களைக் கொண்டு கட்டிய அணை. இது (௧௰௨) யோசனை நிகளம் (௧௰) யோசனை அகலம். இது மூன்று நாட்களில் கட்டி முடித்தது. புண்யஸ்நான கட்டம். இராமேச்சுரத்திற்கும் இலங்கைக்கு முள்ள அணை.

***Setu* in Abithana Chintamani in Tamil, Pg. 1628**

"Rama to vanquish Ravana, to go to Lanka, used Nala a Vanara craftsman Engineer and their Vanara team to build this bridge. This bridge is 120 yojana in length and 10 yojana in width".

Abithana Kosham

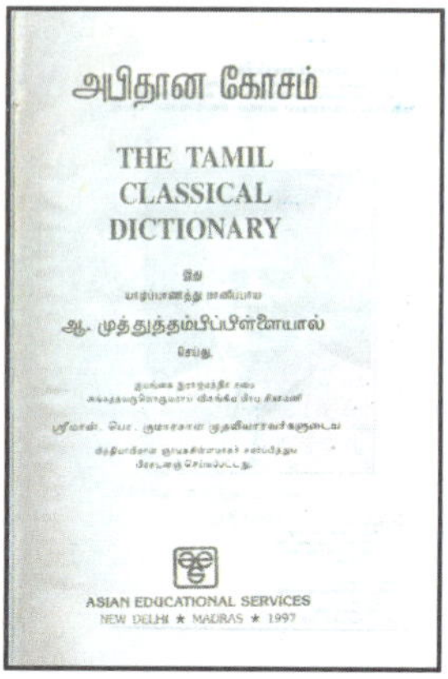

Abithana Kosham - Encyclopaedia from Sri Lanka

P.Coomaraswamy

This was written by A.Muthuthambi Pillaiyal of Sri Lanka in 1902 and dedicated in the Honour of the renowned noble man and scholar, P.Coomaraswamy of Sri Lanka.

An extract of page 168 being,

"From the Pandya Kingdom to Lanka for crossing the seas, Rama and his Vanara sena shovelled the seas and created this path".

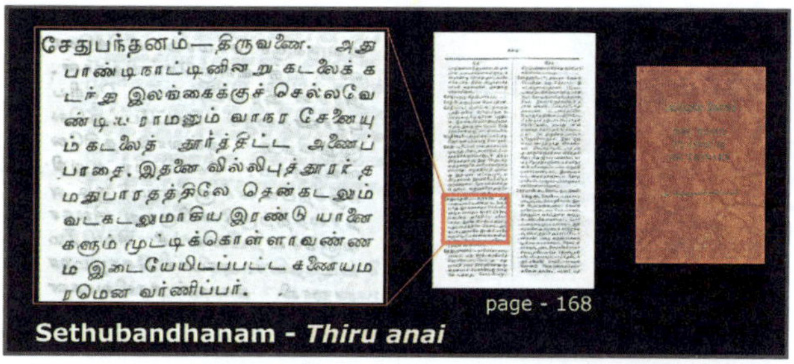

Setubandhanam **- Thiru Anai, Sacred Bridge**

Both these encyclopaedia, show to us, that a bridge across the sea, from India to Lanka, was physically constructed by the *Vanara* team to help Rama. These highlight the historicity of the bridge and the persons involved in its construction, the details of which we shall see as we go further in this book.

The Geographical Trail

RAMAYANA, A GEOGRAPHICALLY CORRECT TEXT

Every site on Rama's route is still identifiable and has continuing traditions in the form of temples and legends to commemorate Rama's visit.

Rama in exile, with wife Sita and brother Lakshmana

All the places visited by Rama still retain memories of His visit.

Some places have commemorative temples while others commemorate Rama's visit in local folklore.

It does not seem plausible that in those remote days, an author would have travelled far and wide to each of those remote places including dense forests and hills to concoct a geographically credible story and build it into local folklore at each of those remote places.

We find a convergence of literature, geography, archaeology and local tradition in this trail.

Let us look at some of the geographical sites, which are popular today due to the events of Ramayana, that unfolded there.

Some popular sites from the period of Ramayana

AYODHYA

Ayodhya is a city in the Northern part of India. It is regarded as the birthplace of Rama. It lies on the banks of the Sarayu River and was ruled by the King Dasaratha, Rama's father, at the time of Rama's birth.

Rama too reigned over this kingdom after His return from the 14 year exile in the forest.

This city has a continuity of history from many thousand years. Various archaeological studies have been undertaken to explore the continuity of the civilization and history of Ayodhya and there have been many debates on the authenticity of the present day Ayodhya, as the birthplace of Rama.

Ayodhya city by the Sarayu River

More on this city of Ayodhya shall be discussed by us in a separate book titled, **"Ayodhya – War and Peace."**

DUNAGIRI

We know from the story of Ramayana, that during the war in Lanka, Lakshmana, the brother of Rama, was mortally wounded. Physician Sushena, who attended to Lakshmana asked for the *Sanjeevani* herb to be brought before the night was through, to revive him. Hanuman was deputed to bring the life saving herb, overnight, before sunrise.

As the story goes, Hanuman searches for the herb in the said part of the Himalayan range but not being able to identify the herb, for paucity of time before the day breaks, he decides to take the whole hillock to the physician Sushena, so that the physician himself could identify and take the needed *Sanjeevani* herb.

Lakshmana mortally wounded at the battlefield

Hanuman carrying the hillock with *Sanjeevani* herbs to Physician Sushena for treating and reviving Lakshmana

Not so well known is the part of the story where, Hanuman returns the hill to its original place, Dunagiri, after use, on the same night, before dawn.

According to this part, Hanuman had promised to the villagers of Dunagiri, that he would return the hillock back in the same place, intact, before dawn. Only on that condition was Hanuman allowed by the villagers of Dunagiri to take the hillock.

Dunagiri is a village in the middle range of Himalayan hills – the Mahabharath range and bears medicinal plants.

Map of India, showing Dunagiri

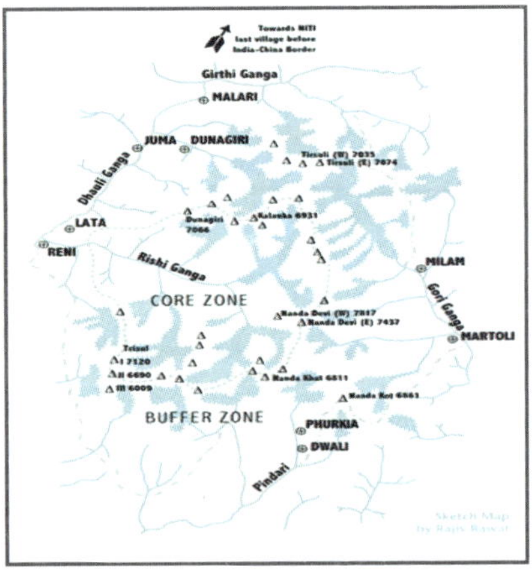

Sketch Map of Dunagiri Region
Courtesy – Rajiv Rawat

According to Dunagiri local folk lore, even today, while Hanuman returned the hillock in time, it was not returned intact.

The Mountains at Dunagiri

As legend goes and local tradition in many places also go, Hanuman spilled parts of the *Sanjeevani* hill all along his trail from the Himalaya to Lanka and back. Hence the whole hillock could not have been returned intact, to its original place as promised by Hanuman to the locals there, before taking the hillock.

Dunagiri mountain slopes, showing a scooped out like appearance considered to be the missing parts of the hill

Because of his failure to keep up his word, the local villagers at Dunagiri, while they offer prayers to Rama and Hanuman, they refuse to take the temple *Prasad,* offerings, during the annual festival of the village, even to this day.

Dunagiri Village

It is interesting to note that one of the medicinal plants on Hanuman's list, *Visalyakarani,* in Samskrt meaning *"remover of spikes and arrows"*, is indeed found in the Dunagiri hills.

At Dunagiri, we see a convergence of literature, history, geography and botany.

DEVAPRAYAG

In the battle at Lanka, Rama kills Ravana, the King of Lanka, for having abducted His wife Sita and brings Sita back to their capital Ayodhya. On return to Ayodhya, Rama is crowned the King of Ayodhya.

Ravana
A Shiva *Bhakta,* devotee

Ravana, the King of Lanka, who was killed by Rama during the battle, was a Shiva *bhakta,* devotee.

Ravana was an exponent of the *Veda.* He was a gifted *Veena* player, who could play the *Sama Veda* on the *Veena,* a stringed instrument. He was also considered to be a *Brahmin,* scholar, because of his scholastic qualities.Rama therefore had to perform *brahmana vadham prayashchitham,* i.e., an atonement for killing a *Brahmin.* Hence after His coronation, He visited Devprayag along with his brother, to atone for having killed a learned scholar Ravana. Devaprayag is in Uttaranchal, in Northern parts of India, in the Himalaya.

Devprayag *Sangam*
Confluence of Rivers
Alaknanda and Ganga

Even today, Devaprayag, in local tradition, continues to be a spot of pilgrimage, for people to offer their tributes to departed souls and ancestors.

Rama Performing Atonement
A Painting depiction

NASIK - PANCHAVATI

When Rama, Sita and Lakshmana were in exile in the Dandakaranya forest, Surpanaka, the sister of Ravana, also happened to travel through these parts.

She was smitten by the handsome Rama and wanted to marry Him. As Rama was already married to Sita, He refused her proposal and Surpanaka then turned towards Lakshmana with her request. When he too declined her proposal, in the altercation that followed, Surpanaka advanced towards Sita with jealousy and Lakshmana to protect Sita, chopped off Surpanaka's nose, who then fled and complained to her brother Ravana.

This place, where Lakshmana cut off Surpanaka's nose, came to be the present city of Nasik, the name *'Nasik'* having its historical origins in the word *'Nas'* meaning 'nose'.

Panchavati

Near Nasik we have a place known as Panchavati, mentioned in the texts too. The name *Panchavati* is derived from *Pancha* meaning 5 and *Vati*, meaning *Vata* or *Peepal* trees. This was a *Peepal* tree grove. The texts says that Rama, Sita and Lakshmana were living in exile here and it was from here that Ravana abducted Sita, after the Surpanaka's nose cut episode.

Today we find a cave labyrinth called Sita *Gufa* which as per local tradition was one of the places of shelter for Rama, Sita and Lakshmana, while in Panchavati.

KISHKINDA

Kishkinda is near Hampi in modern day Karnataka.

Sugreeva, the *Vanara* prince, lived in *Rishyamukha* hills, on the banks of the Pampa Tungabhadra river.

It was here that Rama and Lakshmana, during their search for Sita, met Sugreeva, Hanuman and the rest of the *Vanara* team and with the help of their friendship, Rama crossed over to Lanka and vanquished Ravana, to bring back Sita.

Rama and Lakshmana meeting Sugreeva and his *Vanara* team

In the British records of the Gazette of Bellary district, which is very near the modern day Hampi or Kishkinda of earlier times, the then British Collector had noted that the forest tribes of that area called themselves the *Vanara* people and used Monkey as a symbol in their totem pole and flag.

The Jaina Ramayana also mentions a banner of the *Vanara* called *Vanaradhvaja, Vanara* flag.

The *Vanara* totem in Bellary District Gazetteer

On a separate thread, Anjanadri hills near Hospet, which is close to Kishkinda, is considered as the birthplace of Hanuman or Anjaneya as he is also popularly called.

We see here, a convergence in literature, geography and traditions of the land.

Rama praying to Shivalinga

RAMESWARAM

Rama and the *Vanara* army reached the southern coast of India at a place now known as Rameswaram, to cross the seas to reach Lanka.

Here Rama made a *Shivalinga* out of sand, on the coast and prayed to Shiva, before crossing the seas with the *Vanara* army. This *Shivalinga* and the temple that came up around it, since then, has been called Rameswaram.

Rameswaram Temple

LANKA

After abducting Sita, Ravana took her to his kingdom called Lanka which was across the seas. He kept her captive at the *Ashokavana* also known as *Ashoka Vatika* in Lanka, one of the most beautiful places in his kingdom in the hope that the beautiful surroundings would make Her change Her mind and consent to marry Ravana.

While Sita continued to defy Ravana's advances, Rama's *Vanara* army located Her at Lanka. A bridge was built across the seas to Lanka by the *Vanara* and Rama and the *Vanara* army marched over. After a very fierce battle, they overcame the army of Ravana and vanquished Ravana to bring Sita safely back to Ayodhya.

Sri Lanka of today is considered by both the government as well as locals of Sri Lanka and India, as the Lanka of Ramayana times and just as there are many sites forming a Geographical trail in India of the places connected with the events of Ramayana, Rama and the others of those times, there are atleast 50 sites in Sri Lanka, which claim to bear a connection with Ravana, his clan, Sita and the events of Ramayana which unfolded in Lanka.

For example *Ashoka Vatika* where Sita was held captive is today identified as the place called Sita Eliya. It is identifiable based on the descriptions, local legends and a small monument which has been there since time immemorial to commemorate the occasion.

Sitai Amman Temple at Ashoka Vatika, Nuwara Eliya

This information of Sita Eliya being the spot where Sita was kept prisoner has been bought forth by Donald Obeyesekera one of the respected historians of Sri Lanka in the last century. Donald Obeyasekera's work highlights the geographical areas of Sita's stay in Lanka.

"The purity of Sita's character and her devotion to her husband have made her the national heroine.

Sita's name lives in Sita-talawa (Sita's plain), Sita-ela (Sita's stream) and Sita-kunt (Sita's pond) between Nuwara Eliya and Hakgala, where she is said to have been confined by Ravana and in Sitawaka (Avisawella)." -an extract from **Outlines of Ceylon History** by Donald Obeyesekera.

Apart from these geographical locations, there are some more interesting pointers in the topography and geography of Sri Lanka which vindicate its association with the times of Rama, Ravana and Ramayana.

More on the events of Ramayana in Lanka, is covered in our work, **"Ramayana In Lanka."**

ADAM'S BRIDGE – NALA *SETU*

Satellite image of bridge connecting Danushkodi in India with Thalaimannar in Sri Lanka

Rama and the *Vanara* had to cross the sea to reach Lanka and fight Ravana to being back Sita. The Ramayana story clearly speaks of the construction of a bridge across the sea, by the *Vanara* army. Whilst this structure has been mentioned in various texts, many times over, nobody else in Indian history or any other literature has claimed its construction nor has referred to it other than as a bridge built by Rama and the *Vanara* team.

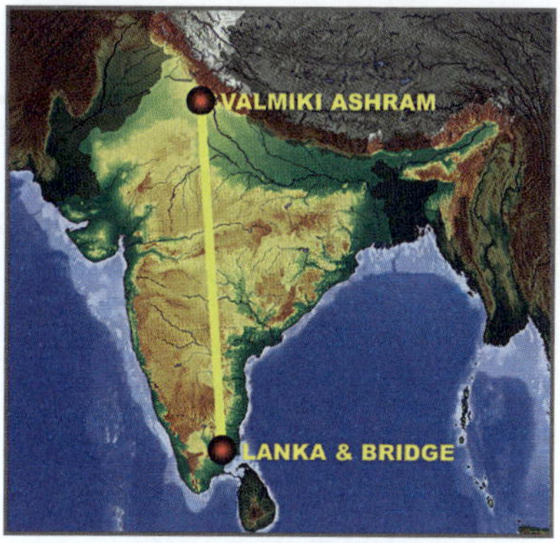

Where Valmiki lived, Lanka and the bridge

Though Valmiki did not visit the south, his description of the various places enroute from Kishkinda to the sea coast and beyond to Lanka, is accurate and verifiable to this day.

There are some, who have opinioned and have postulated, that all the events of Ramayana including that in Lanka took place in Central India itself, and the crossing of the seas may have been the crossing of a river in central India.

Valmiki in his description has clearly mentioned the Nala *Setu* as a bridge built across the seas. Going by his accurate descriptions of the rest of the topography in both India and Lanka, Valmiki would surely have known the difference between a sea and a river.

All the geographical descriptions mentioned by Valmiki, are clearly verifiable across the land of Lanka and India, even today.

BHARATHA'S RETURN FROM KEKEYA TO AYODHYA

Bharatha was a brother of Rama. As per the wishes of Bharatha's mother Kaikeyi, their father, King Dasaratha was coerced into ordering his favourite son Rama, into the forest on a 14 year exile and declaring Bharatha as the crown prince.

However, King Dasaratha, overcome by the grief of having been compelled to order his favourite and worthy son Rama into the forest, died soon after, leaving the Kingdom to Bharatha.

During the course of all these events, Bharatha was at his maternal grandfather's house in Kekaya. He was therefore summoned to perform his father's last rites and ascend the throne.

Bharatha's return travel from Kekeya to Ayodhya, is described in detail in the Ramayana text, along with the description of the rivers he crosses enroute.

"Bharatha started his journey in the easterly direction. Crossed the Sudama river first and then the Sutudri river, which flows towards west. Thereafter, he crossed mighty hills and then reached the Saraswati and Ganga river. Subsequently, he reached the Kingdom of Matsya and from there travelled in a northerly direction, on his way to Ayodhya."

- Valmiki Ramayana - 2.71.1-5

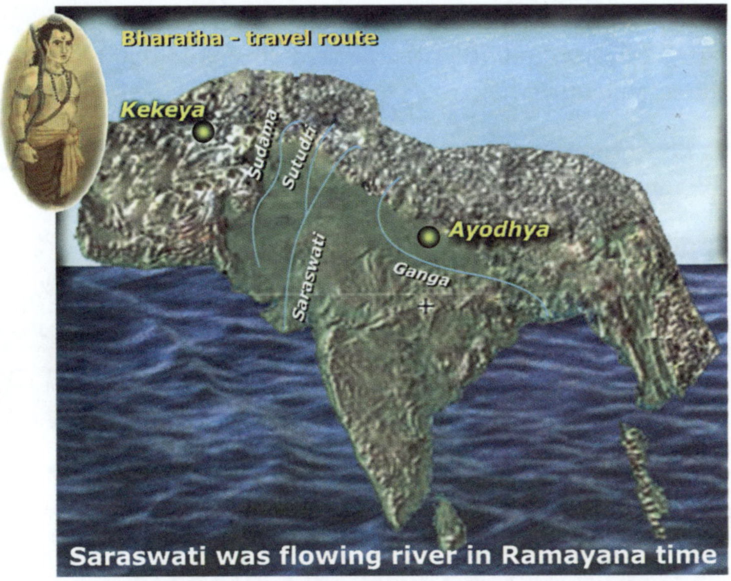

Bharatha's Travel Route from Kekeya to Ayodhya

The rivers are mentioned here in the same order in which they are found while approaching Ayodhya from the Northwest of India, today. From the rivers mentioned here, we may conclude that Kekeya was a region beyond Afghanistan. We may also note that one of the rivers mentioned here is the Saraswati river.

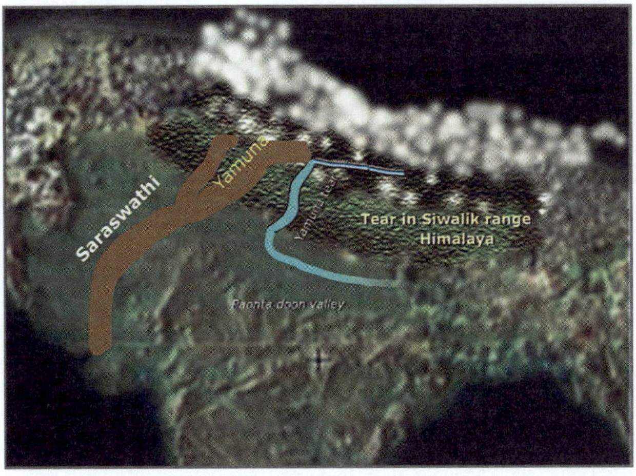

Saraswati River going dry, tear in Siwalik Range of Himalaya

This Sarsawati river, which was flowing in the north west of India, through Haryana and Rajasthan, went dry over 4500 years back, due to tectonic movements.

This is now borne out by the satellite image of the Yamuna tear of the Siwalik range of the Himalaya.

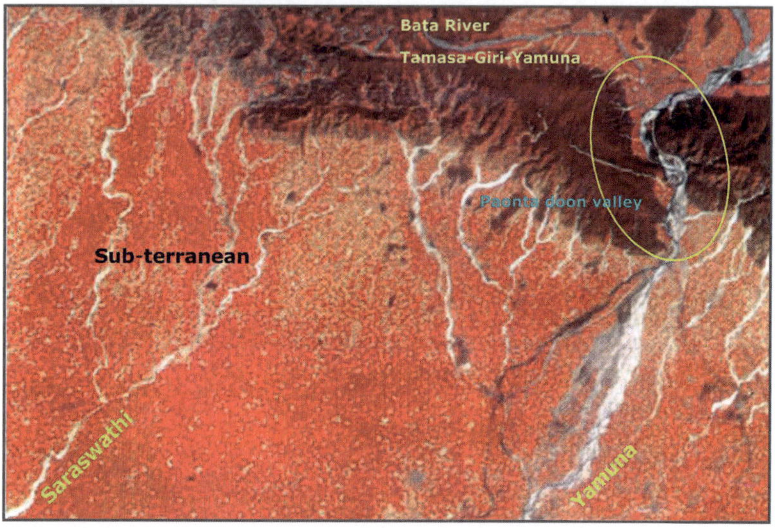

Yamuna Tear 2500 BCE

Since the description of Bharatha's travel describes him as having crossed a flowing Saraswati river, it implies that the events of Ramayana should have taken place before Saraswati went dry, i.e., atleast 5000 years ago or much earlier than that, when the Saraswati was a flowing river.

This proves that the events of Ramayana, are atleast over 5000 years old and could well be much older than that as well.

SUGREEVA SENDS A SEARCH PARTY

Sugreeva sends his *Vanara* in all directions, in search of Sita.

Sugreeva's instruction to them is as follows:

"You Search for Sita, on and around the banks of Bhagirathi, Sarayu, Kaushiki, Kalindi, Yamuna, Saraswati, Sindhu, Sone, Mahi and Kaalmahi rivers".

- Valmiki Ramayana, 4.40.20-22

Sugreeva instructing the *Vanara* to search in all directions
A palm leaf sketch

This instruction of Sugreeva, tells us that in the times of Ramayana, the river Saraswati was a flowing river of those times and was considered a big enough river to find mention in his instructions. This again pre antiquates the Ramayana, to before the drying of the Saraswati river or to atleast more than 5000 years ago.

KUMARI KANDAM

Sugreeva dispatches another set of *Vanara* to the South and instructs them to search for Sita in the following locations -

"Search the Malayagir mountains, you will find Rishi Agastya there, then cross Kaveri river, then cross Tamaraparani river, then you will see the Golden Door of Kapada puram, Capital of Pandya Kings,"

- Valmiki Ramayanam
- Kishkinda Khandam Chapter 41 - Sloka 14-18

Kapadapuram the town mentioned as reference here by Sugreeva, was a celebrated town of the 2nd Tamil *Sangam* period. This town is now submerged in the Sea as per the Tamil *Sangam* texts.

This period in Tamil literature was atleast, about 4000 years ago and probably more.

This cross reference also places the Ramayana to be over 4000 years and more old.

This cross reference also vindicates the geographies mentioned in both the Valmiki Ramayana and the Tamil Sangam texts, as they were two independent texts written by different authors, in very different but ancient languages of the world.

Archaeo-Astronomy

A NEW WAY OF DATING

Archaeo-Astronomy is a new term comprising of 2 components. Archaeo derived from archaic and Astronomy, the science of sky observations. The subject Archaeo-Astronomy deals with a new way of utilizing science to study the archaic.

This is a technique of charting the future or past sky using a scientific tool. This tool helps to arrive at planetary positions given a date in future or past and vice-versa i.e., given a set of planetary configurations, the tool can help identify the date in future when the planetary configuration could occur or identify the date in the past, when the planetary configuration could have occurred.

Such tools are collectively called Planetarium software. There are probably over 50 such different software available to us and can be bought off the shelf. Each software, is typically used for a particular application, such as plotting the current night sky chart or predicting eclipses and the likes.

In the last decade or so, NASA has been regularly sending space missions such as Voyager I & II to the outer planets. It takes about 10 to 12 years for the spacecraft to reach the outer planets such as Saturn, Jupiter and Uranus. For the spacecraft to reach the orbit of the respective planet correctly, planetary positions have to be calculated precisely. The space agencies have therefore come up with software that work based on an extremely accurate and precise understanding of the revolution speed of these planets and other stellar bodies, their orbits, earth's rotation, its axis, its orbit etc.

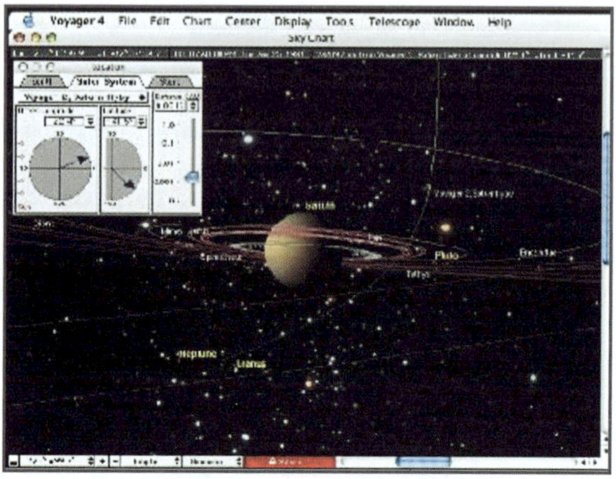

Planetarium software

These software have now become declassified and available for public use as Planetarium software.

Such a software can be utilized by us today in an innovative manner, to give specific dates to the events mentioned in the Indian legends.

Unlike any other civilization so far, the literature of the Indian civilization is characterized for being embedded with night sky observations. Feeding the observations of the planetary configurations into the Planetarium software or even performing tedious manual calculations can give us the Gregorian calendar dates when these configurations could have occurred in the past. When these dates are found to be logically arranged with respect to the events, it helps us to scientifically assign dates to the events mentioned in the Indian legends and historical texts.

Rishi observing the night sky

Thus the astronomical descriptions available to us in our literature can be analyzed scientifically to arrive at historic dates for the various events mentioned therein. This approach, which gives rise to a new branch of scientific dating based on Astronomy, is parallel to Archaeology where physical remains are analyzed to arrive at historic dates and hence may be called Archaeo-Astronomy.

This technique of dating – Archaeo-Astronomy is still not widely accepted or practiced by many orthodox historians as it requires knowledge of traditional astronomy, mathematics as well modern day sky chart reading techniques, all of which go into the realm of science. This technique of dating requires and will create a new breed of historians. It has the potential to date more events from our vast store of literature.

DATING RAMAYANA

Various modern day researchers have made use of the Planetarium software to arrive at historic dates for various events described in the Indian literature.

However, even prior to the arrival of this software, many researchers, proficient in astronomy and literature, have performed tedious manual calculations based on the planetary configurations in the text and arrived at the dates for legendary heroes such as Rama and Krishna and events in Ramayana and Mahabharatha respectively.

We collated and examined the works of many that are credible and worthy of standing up to due examination.

In the context of the Historicity of Rama, the work of Shri. Pushkar Bhatnagar, as brought out in his book **"Dating the Era of Lord Ram"**, forms the basis of what is presented here to understand the dates of the events in Rama's lifetime.

Pushkar Bhatnagar

In the Ramayana text, in a few places, embedded in the dialogues of the characters, Valmiki has mentioned in passing, the details of the night sky and other astral events. These have been carefully culled out and when the software is used to search the skies for the same configuration, the software throws up the dates when that particular sky configuration could have occurred in the past. There are more than a handful of events in the story of Ramayana, where clear astronomical references are given.

Some of these events are discussed here along with the skychart, i.e., the view of the sky that day, as shown by the Planetarium Software. These skycharts show the various stellar constellations in the form of lines connecting stars to form the various constellation patterns. The vertices of these lines are the stars.

Various odd shaped closed boxes, enclosing each such line pattern, denote the expanse of the sky which is considered to be the region of that constellation.

The planets, sun and moon can be found within the respective constellation areas, as indicated by the Ramayana text. Examining the skycharts to see this correlation, makes for an interesting exercise.

SRI RAM NAVAMI – BIRTH OF RAMA

Sri Rama Navami is celebrated as the birth day of Rama as He was born on the *Navami thithi* of *Shukla Paksha* of *Chaitra masa,* i.e., the 9th day of the increasing phase of the moon, in the lunar month of *Chaitra.*

At that time, the nakshatra was Punarvasu and Sun, Mars, Saturn, Jupiter and Venus were in Aries, Capricorn, Libra, Cancer and Pisces respectively. Lagna was Cancer and Jupiter & Moon were shining together.

- Ramayana 1.18.8,9

This *sloka* has been used by many astrologers to eulogize about the qualities of Rama and showcase from an astrological perspective, the reasons why Rama went through various hardships in life.

The same *sloka,* can also be used for astronomically dating the birth of Rama in the Gregorian calendar.

Birth of Rama

For this purpose, the star positions can be summarized as follows for our easy understanding:

1. Sun in Aries
2. Saturn in Libra
3. Jupiter in Cancer
4. Venus in Pisces
5. Mars in Capricorn
6. Lunar month of *Chaitra*
7. 9th day after New Moon, i.e., *Navami Thithi, Shukla Paksha*
8. Moon near *Punarvasu Nakshatra,* Pollux star in Gemini constellation.
9. Cancer as *Lagna,* i.e., Cancer constellation rising in the east.
10. Jupiter above the horizon

The observations when searched using a Planetarium software gives us the following Sky Chart, which in turn gives forth the date for *Sri Rama Navami* as 10th January 5114 BCE, at 12.30 p.m. in the afternoon.

Skychart for the Birth of Rama - 10th January 5114 BCE

BIRTH OF BHARATHA

Similarly, the sky configuration during Bharatha's birth, when searched using the Planetarium software, gives a Sky Chart of Bharatha's birth as follows.

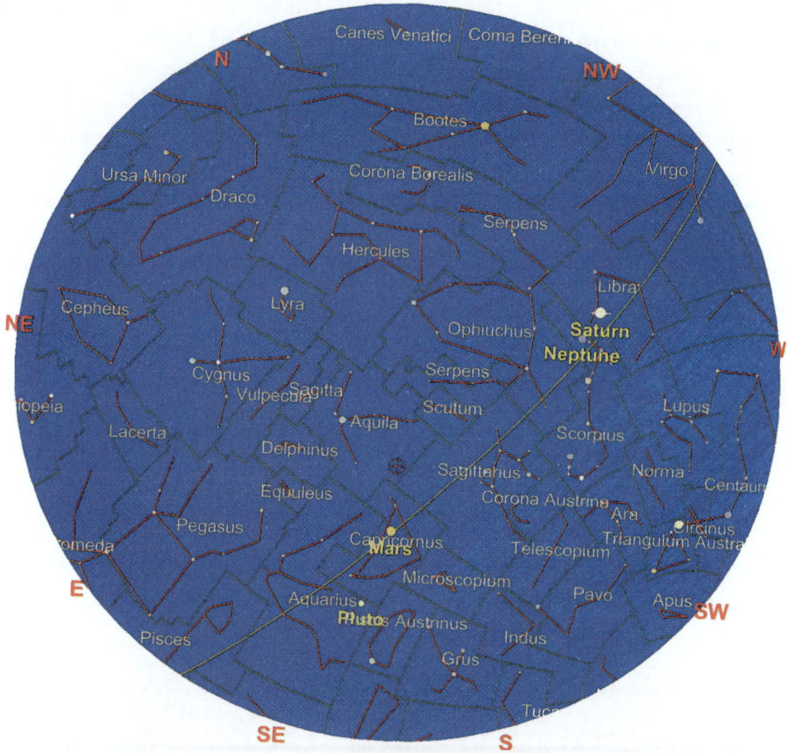

Birth of Bharatha - 11th January 5114 BCE, 4.30 a.m.

From the previous sky chart of Rama's birth, we can see that this is about 16 hours after birth of Rama.

In the Ramayana text too, it is clearly mentioned that Bharatha was born 16 hours after Rama.

CORONATION EVE

Rama and His brothers were born to King Dasaratha, quite late in life, after much penance, *yagna.*

When Rama had reached the age to be made the *Yuvaraja,* crown prince, King Dasaratha, called in his courtiers, to express his intention to crown Rama as the Crown Prince. In these discussions, Dasaratha mentions the month, the planetary positions and expresses concern that they were malefic to him.

Fearing this, King Dasaratha, prefers to anoint Rama as his successor and the Crown Prince, before something befalls him.

While the later events may have proven this fear to be true, the astrological predictions are not the focus here. We would like to see if the planetary configurations mentioned here in the text can help us arrive at the date when the event must have occurred.

King Dasaratha with his Courtiers

King Dasaratha to his courtiers –

"This month of Chaitra is beautiful and holy. The woods and trees are full of flowers. At this time coronation of Rama is most appropriate."

- Ramayana 2.4.21-22

The month is *Chaitra*. In present understanding, it is the month before the onset of summer.

King Dasaratha summons Rama and expresses his intention to Rama.

King Dasaratha with Rama

"Astrologers have told me that my nakshatra has been surrounded by malefic planets like Sun, Mars and Rahu. Under such planetary configurations, the king either dies or falls in some deep conspiracy. Thus, before I face any such problem, you take over the kingship".

- Ramayana 2.4.18

The *Rasi,* Zodiac sign, for King Dasaratha was Pisces. So, as per this *Sloka,* Sun, Mars and *Rahu* node, were in the Pisces constellation, during this conversation.

"Today the moon is on Punarvasu nakshatra and tomorrow it will meet the Pushya nakshatra. In that Pushya nakshatra, I am eager to hand over the kingdom to you."

- Ramayana 2.4.21-22

This indicates that the Moon was transiting from the star *Punarvasu* to *Pushya* as part of its monthly 28 day transit from one Zodiac constellation to another.

If we enter these parameters in the planetarium software and look for when this star configuration must have occurred in the sky, then we get to the star chart and the date as, 4th January 5089 BCE.

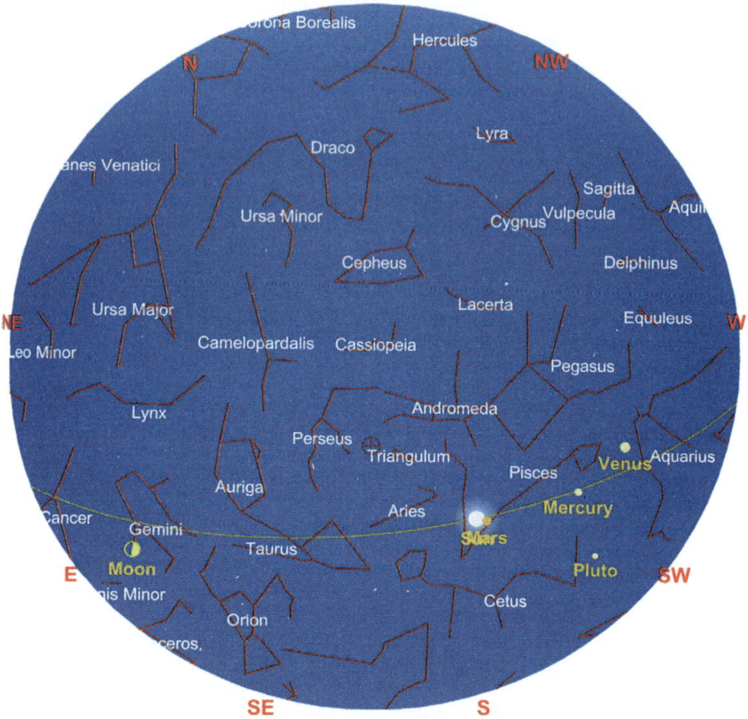

Planets located together in Pisces constellation 4th January 5089 BCE Coronation Eve

The elapse time between this date and Rama's birth is 25 years. So Rama was 25 years when He was sent on Exile. This tallies well with the internal textual information of the text.

KHAR - DUSHAN EPISODE

Rama, His wife Sita and brother Lakshmana were to live in the forest, *Vanavasa*, as a part of their 14 year exile. While they were roaming in the Dandakaranya forest, Surpanaka, the sister of the mighty *Rakshasa* King, Ravana, the king of Lanka, sees Rama and takes a liking to Him. Wanting to marry Rama, she proposes to Rama. Rama not interested in her advances, suggests she propose to Lakshmana, His brother, who also rejects her proposal.

The spurned woman Surpanaka, then turns violent and goes to attack the demure Sita. Lakshmana, who had accompanied Rama and Sita, to guard them while in exile in the forest, cuts off the nose of the intruding Surpanaka, as was the norm of punishment in vogue then for adultery or improper advances. More on this can be found in our book **Ramayana in Lanka** in the Bharath Gyan Series.

Lakshmana chopping off Surpanaka's nose

Surpanaka, immediately rushes to her brothers Khar and Dushan who lived in the nearby forest, to engage Rama and Lakshmana in a fight, to avenge her nose cut.

Khar and Dushan advance towards Rama for a fight. A wordy duel precedes their fight.

The conversation of the wordy duel, gives us very interesting insights into the sky configuration for that day, the solar eclipse that was to occur then and the array of planets that were visible in the afternoon sky, during the eclipse period.

Khar tells Rama -

"I want to say many things about my prowess but I would not, because if in the meanwhile sunset occurs, there would be a break in the battle."

- Ramayana: 3.29.23

Rama and Lakshmana, fighting Khar and Dhushan

Khar wants to speak about himself more, but says, he has to resist himself, as he wants to start the fight before the premature sunset due to the eclipse that was to start.

The description of the Solar Eclipse is given in the following texts as:

"When Khar moved with his army towards Rama for the battle, a red coloured evening appeared to be descending all over."

- Ramayana 3.23.1

"The Sun was covered by a dark coloured disc that had red coloured corners."

- Ramayana 3.23.3

"Although it was daytime, it started appearing to be evening."

- Ramayana 3.23.9

"The Sun was caught by Rahu because of which the Sun lost its glow and brightness.

Various animals and birds started making noises as if was dusk."

- Ramayana 3.23.12

"In the middle of his army, Khar was looking like Mars in the middle of the planets in the sky."

- Valmiki Ramayana

The pointers we can draw from the above *sloka* are:

- Planets, visible to unaided eyes were from the East to West - Saturn, Sun, Moon, Mars, Mercury, Venus, and Jupiter.
- Mars was in the middle of this chain.
- Rarely, all the planets are in the day sky.
- Rarer is Mars in the middle of them.
- The occurrence of a solar eclipse at that time makes it absolutely unique.

These are some of the rarest of the rare astronomical events, which got recorded because of their uniqueness. Mars is rarely seen in the middle of a planetary alignment.

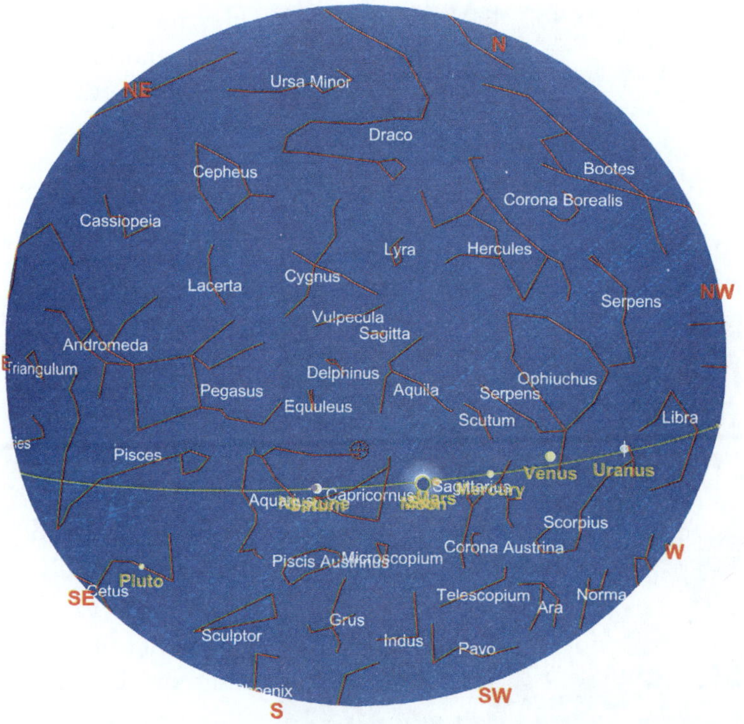

Sky chart for the day of Eclipse at Panchavati - 7th October 5077 BCE

The Sky Chart shows the configuration at 2.00 p.m. with the Latitude/Longitude for Panchavati, Nasik, the place where Surpanaka's nose was chopped off by Lakshmana.

The Sky chart shows that a Solar eclipse on 7th October 5077 BCE, did indeed reach maximum coverage at Panchavati at 15.10 hours tallying well with the literature.

THE SLAYING OF VALI, *VALI VADHAM*

After Rama loses Sita, He wanders in the forest along with Lakshmana, searching for Sita. During the course of that wandering, He reaches *Rishyamukha* mountains in central India where He befriends Sugreeva and his lieutenant Hanuman, who have with them the ornaments that were dropped by Sita, when She was being abducted by Ravana.

Dying Vali, paying his respects to Rama

Hearing the story of Rama and His lost wife Sita, Sugreeva offers to help Rama, in searching and bringing back Sita, provided Rama first helps Sugreeva in getting back at Vali, his elder brother, who had unjustly exiled him and also detained Sugreeva's wife, against her wishes. Sugreeva seeks help from Rama as Vali was mightier than Sugreeva.

Rama enters into a pact with Sugreeva wherein Sugreeva calls Vali for a fight and Rama, hiding in the bushes, shoots an arrow and strikes Vali down.

In describing the death of Vali, a simile is given, in which we can infer that there was a solar eclipse at that time.

"Hearing the roar of Sugreeva, Vali's face became red like the sun caught by Rahu during the eclipse."

- Ramayana 4.15.3

Vali – Sugreeva fight with Rama in the bushes – a Sculpture

Plotting the data in the planetarium software and looking for a solar eclipse in the morning hours in Central India, we do indeed see that an eclipse did occur in Kishkinda on 3rd April, 5076 BCE.

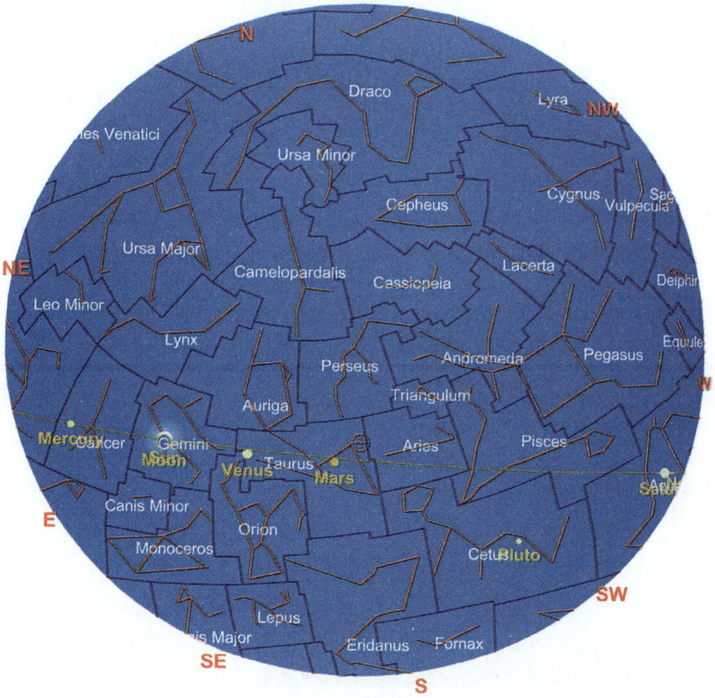

Sky chart when Vali was slayed – 3rd April 5076 BCE

"Vali Vadham", the slaying of Vali, thus occurred on 3rd April, 5076 BCE, during the Solar Eclipse, on *Amavasya*, New Moon day of the month of *Ashada*, during the morning hours.

HANUMAN'S VISIT TO LANKA

Sugreeva despatched a number of search parties to different parts of the land to locate the whereabouts of Sita.

In one such search party, deputed to the South, was Hanuman. Hanuman crossed over the seas in the southern part of India to reach Lanka. There he found Sita in *Ashokavana* grove, having a forlorn look. The description of the look and state of Sita, is beautifully intertwined in the story, with the occurrence of a partial Lunar eclipse, during their meeting.

Hanuman found Sita looking like a full moon which was eclipsed by Rahu.

- Ramayana 5.10.14

Sita's face looked like a full moon that had just been released from Rahu's captivity. (released from an eclipse)

- Ramayana 5.29.7

Sita's face resembled the full moon released from the grip of Rahu.

- Ramayana 5.35.87

Hanuman finds Sita

With this information, when we look for such an eclipse, which could have been seen from Lanka in the early part of the night, we do notice that such an eclipse did occur on 12th September, 5076 BCE.

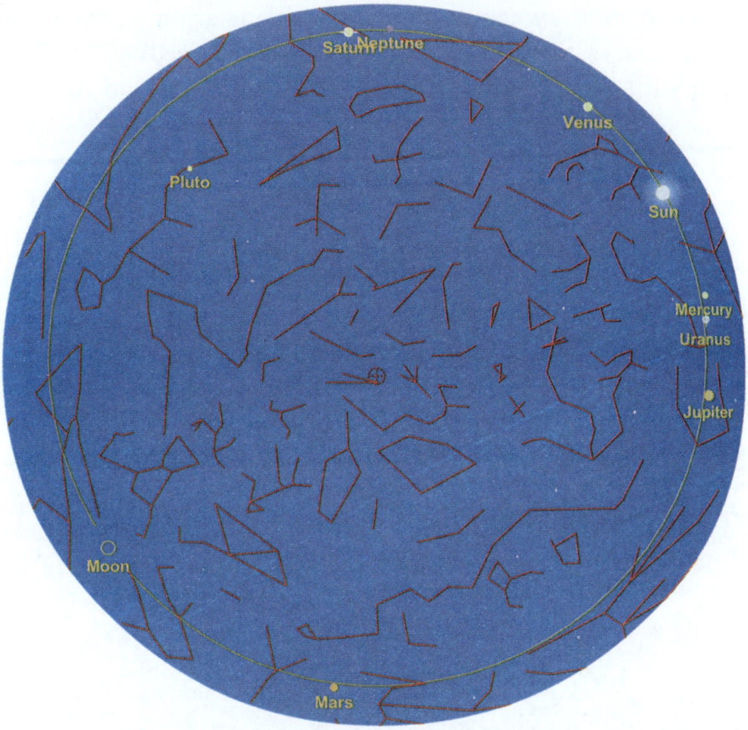

Hanuman's Visit to Lanka - 12th September 5076 BCE - Lunar Eclipse

The eclipsed moon rose in the eastern sky. It was not a total lunar eclipse. The place of observation is Lanka.

HANUMAN'S RETURN FROM LANKA

Hanuman, after meeting Sita and going on a rampage over the capital city of Lanka and setting it on fire, returns back across the sea, to where his other friends of the search party were waiting for him.

During this return journey, Hanuman observes the stars in the early morning sky, which are mentioned in a sloka in the Ramayana text.

- The Sun and Moon are shining together.
- Mars and Jupiter are shining.
- Also seen are *Pushya* Cancer, *Swati* Virgo, *Airavat* elephant of *Indra* corresponding to Scorpio.

These observations, when plotted in the Planetarium software, show these star observations to be of the morning succeeding, Hanuman's meeting with Sita, thus validating both these events and their dates, which were arrived at independently.

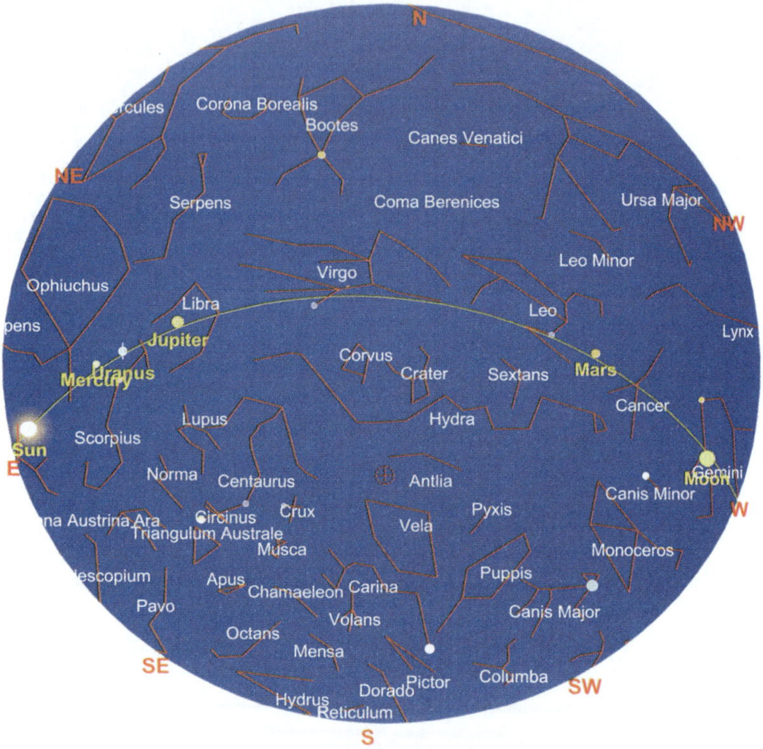

Hanuman's Return from Lanka - 14th September 5076 BCE
Observation at 6.30 a.m.

START OF THE ARMY MARCH

Having identified the place where Sita had been held captive, Hanuman returns to his capital Kishkinda and informs Rama and Sugreeva, of how Ravana was holding Sita in captivity. Sugreeva garners his *Vanara* army to march southwards from his capital Kishkinda, towards Lanka.

Before embarking on their journey for the battle, they look for the right omens, for the army to start their march. The discussions around these omens are useful for us today, to clearly date the start of the army march.

Rama says-

"Today the sun has already risen to the middle of the sky and this is the famous Vijay Mahurath. In my opinion we must start our journey towards Lanka in this Vijay Mahurath, to win the battle against Ravana."

- Ramayana 6.4.3

"Today is Uttara - Phalguni Nakshatra and tomorrow the moon would meet the Hasta Nakshatra. O Sugreeva! We must start our journey immediately along with the army of Vanara."

- Ramayana 6.4.6

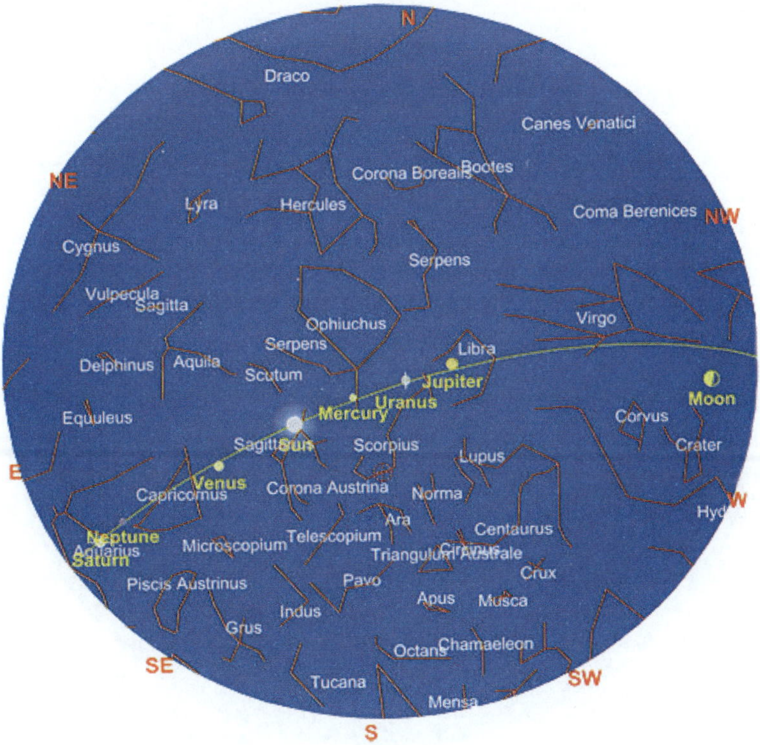

Start of the Army March to Lanka - 19th September 5076 BCE

VANARA ARMY MARCHING TO LANKA

Vanara **army marching towards Lanka**

As the army continues to march towards Lanka, Lakshmana observes the sky position, to see if it augured well for them, as they were going to battle. This observation helps us in plotting it in the Planetarium software to understand the date of the march of the army.

Lakshmana's observation : *"Venus has gone to the back side, Sapta-rishi* (Ursa Major) *are visible brightly, Trishanku* (Crux) *our ancestor, is visible in front. Moola nakshatra, protector of Rakshasa, is being inflicted with Dhumra-ketu* (node)."

- Ramayana 6.4.48-50

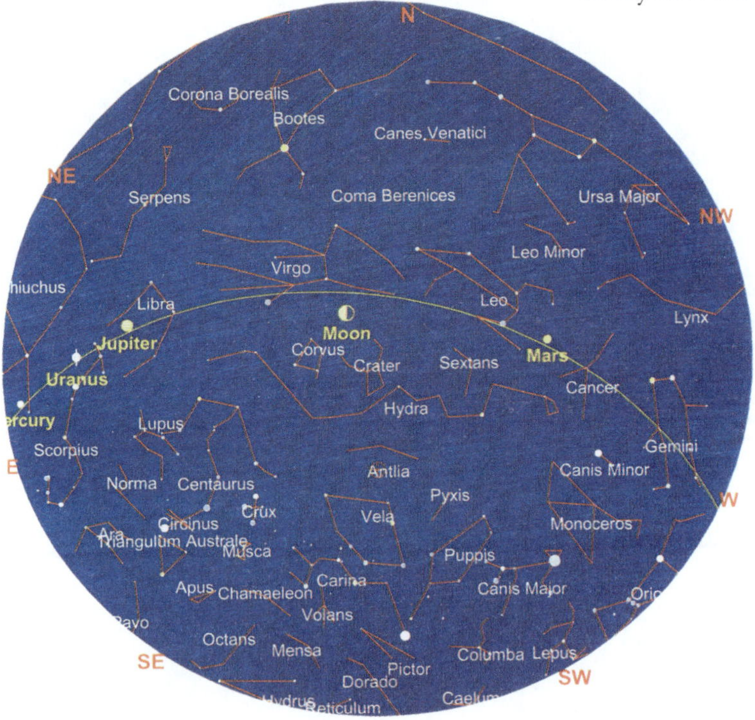

The *Vanara* Army marching to Lanka - 20th September, 5076 BCE

ARMY REACHES RAVANA'S FORT

The *Vanara* Army reached the final location – the fort of Ravana on *"Suvael"* hill after crossing the seas.

"When the army reached the fort located on the hill called 'Suvael', the full moon night occurred at the end of the Pausha month."

- Ramayana 6.38.19

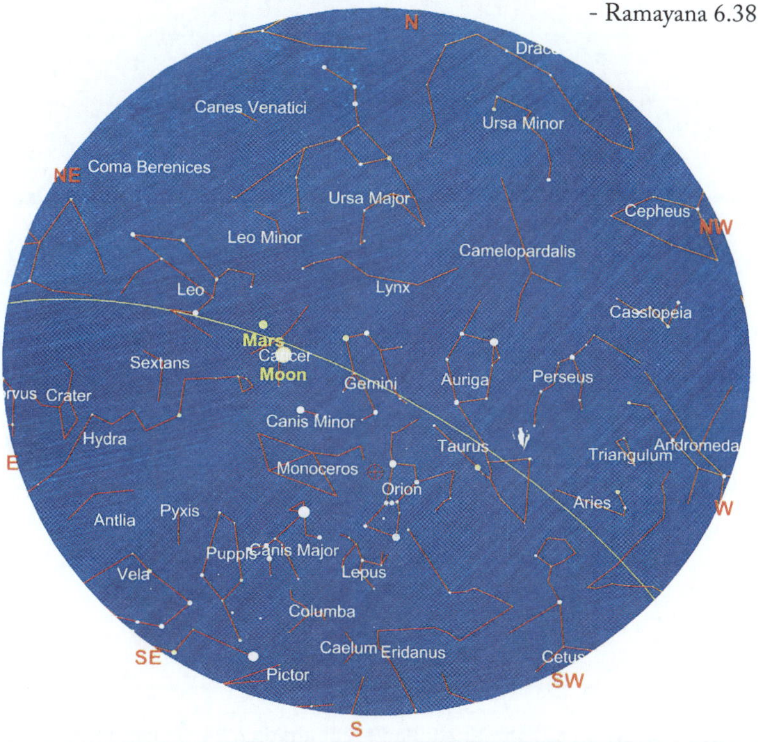

Sky chart of night the *Vanara* army reach Ravana Fort
12th October, 5076 BCE

When plotted using the software, we find this to have happened on the full moon night of 12th October, 5076 B.C.E.

DEATH OF MEGHANADA

In the fierce battle at Lanka, Lakshmana, the brother of Rama, kills Meghanada - the illustrious son of Ravana. In the description of the fight between them, the position of the moon is mentioned, which helps us now determine the date on which Meghanada was slayed by Lakshmana, as, 24th November, 5076 B.C.E.

"Lakshmana killed Meghanada, after 3 continuous days of battle, on the 14th day of the decreasing phase of moon. One day before Amavasya."

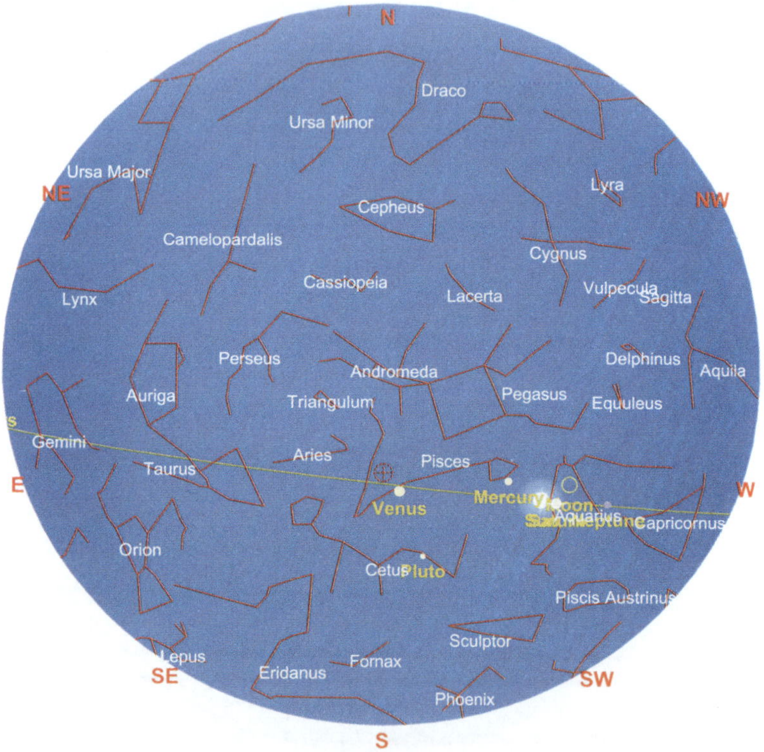

Star position when Lakshmana killed Meghanada - 24th November, 5076 BCE

A depiction of Lakshmana killing Meghanada

AN INTERNAL CONSISTENCY

We have seen over the last few pages, a series of observations, as mentioned in the Valmiki Ramayana text. Plotting all of them in the Planetarium software, helps arrive at individual, independent dates for each one of these events.

What would now be interesting to see is if all these dates that have been arrived at individually, are in the same sequence as they occur in the unfolding of the events of the Ramayana story.

For, if even one of the dates identified, does not tally with the same sequence of events as per the text, then the whole effort would be a waste.

What is amazing is that, the whole sequence of dates, as thrown up by the planetarium software follows the same sequence of the events of the story as per the text, making the dates internally consistent and thus proving the historicity of the events of Ramayana.

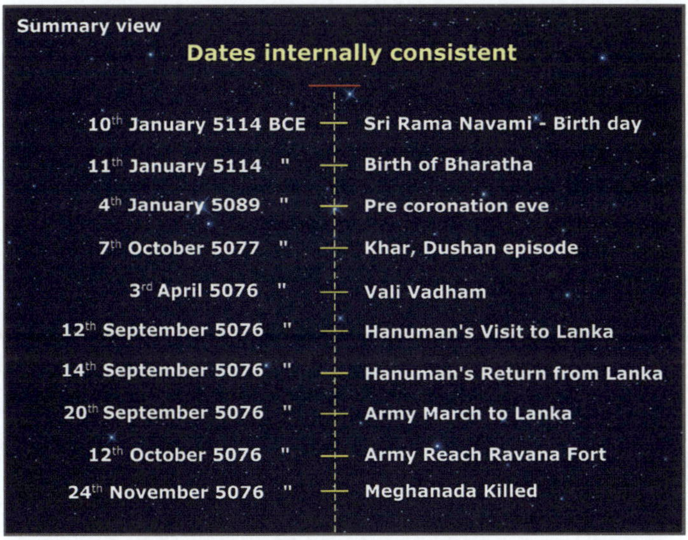

Internal consistency of all dates

Not only are the dates mentioned by the Planetarium software important, what is even more important, is the internal consistency of the dates.

It may be noted from the table above that the dates arrived at for the events are not haphazard. They tally with the chronological sequence for the events as found in the Ramayana text.

Not only that, the elapse times between the events too, as indicated by these dates also tally with the elapse-time and duration or age as described by Valmiki, in the Ramayana text. This establishes internal consistency in these dates and proves the credibility of the technique.

CROSS VALIDATION OF DATES

Closing the Gap

Sri Rama Navami – The Birthday of Rama now occurs around the 21st of April, in the month of *Chaithra.* During the days of Rama, i.e., in 5114 BCE, the *Navami* (9th day of the lunar cycle) of *Chaithra* month had occurred on the 10th of January. Here, between the years 5114 BCE and 2010 CE, we see a difference of 100 days between the occurrence of *Navami* in the *Chaithra* month.

How does one account for this difference of 100 days?

To answer this question we need to understand an astronomical concept now known as Precession of Equinox. While this is a relatively new term, used in modern astronomy, this concept was not unknown to the ancient astronomers of India.

Infact, they had understood the concept of Precession of Equinox, discussed it in their books on astronomy and even suggested correction factors that needed to be applied so that the calendar does not create such wide gaps over years. Among the many such astronomers, Varahamihira, the noted astronomer and mathematician too, has mentioned about it.

Varahamihira's Brihad Samhita

The Brihad Samhita compiled by Varahamihira around 530 CE states that, the Retrograde Motion of the Vernal Equinox *(Vasant Sampat)* is 1° in 72 years - i.e., there is a slide of 1 day for every 72 years.

Varahamihira

Varahamihira also goes on to suggest that a correction factor be applied every 500 years to overcome this.

Precession of Equinox

Modern day astronomers have termed this slide as Precession of equinox and state that it is 1 day in every 72 years.

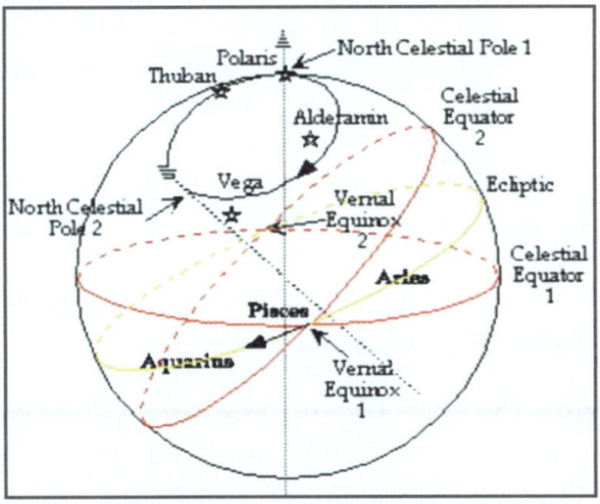

Precession of Equinox

Taking cue from Varahamihira, as well as the modern concept of precession of equinox, if a slide of 1 day occurs in 72 years, then a slide of 100 days would need 7200 years of elapse time.

The difference between 5114 BCE and 2010 CE is 7124 years which is indeed very close to 7200 years. This proves that 10th January, 5114 BCE is a highly probable date for the birth of Rama.

OTHER SCHOLARLY EFFORT

You may ask, "Why has Bharath Gyan taken the work of Shri.Pushkar Bhatnagar as the most probable date for the events of Ramayana?

Are there others who have done similar work, in astronomically dating the events of Ramayana?"

In fact, there have been a series of respected, well read scholars over the last few decades who have astronomically tried to date the events of Ramayana. Some of these scholars include,

- Prof. K.S. Raghavan - Madras
- Dr. P.V. Vartak - Pune
- Sri P.V. Mendki - Kalyan
- Sri Narsing Rao
- Sri N.P. Ramadurai – Thanjavur

We salute their pioneering effort. Each one of them have used tools and techniques available to them, at their times, to date the events of Rama.

All these persons and more have been the forerunners in this bold effort of astronomically dating the events of Ramayana.

We feel that it is the culmination of all their efforts, which has led us today, to date Rama, at 5114 BCE.

The work of Shri.Pushkar Bhatnagar, using Planetarium Software, seemed more plausible, as it displayed a higher level of internal consistency and also tallied with the other data we had come across from other fields such as geography, oceanography and also from our research on the knowledge of India from various perspectives.

Archaeology

WHERE TO LOOK?

One of the ways of proving historicity today is to show archaeological proof. But a continuous civilization, which India is, while a marvel by itself, does not leave intact, sufficient archaeological remnants of its ancestors. Generations come and go and as they keep building and rebuilding their cities, they destroy or alter the remains of older structures, in order to build newer ones. Hence while the continuous civilizations and their culture, stories and tradition are themselves an evidence, archaeological artefacts are hard to come by.

To understand this, think of a clock which stopped ticking during an earthquake. If nobody repaired it and left it as is, it stands witness to the time of the quake. But if it were to continue ticking, then the clock ceases to be an evidence.

Today, small occasional finds in deserted places are all what we have, to attempt to learn about our ancient history.

It is because the deep seas swallowed Dwaraka, that the town became uninhabitable and frozen in time and hence, after so many thousands of years, it is still able to provide evidence for the existence of an advanced township, tallying with the city described in the epic Mahabharatha.

The only such uninhabited place to look for evidences of Rama's times, as per the epic Valmiki Ramayana, would therefore be to study the Rama *Setu* or Adam's Bridge.

Shri B.B. Lal, Director General, Retd., Archaeological Survey of India, states:

"No contemporary inscriptional evidence is available to establish the historicity of the epic. An advantage in approaching this problem is, the sites mentioned in the epic, bear same names even today. This is because these sites have remained under continuous occupation ever since the 1st settlement began thereat. Authenticity of the names is there, as there is only one Mathura, Hastinapura, Ayodhya, Chitrakoota."

Since traditional archaeological evidences are not directly available due to an elapse time of more than 7200 years, coupled with a continuous civilization, the bridge is probably the only archaeological evidence!

The *Setu* being built by the *Vanara*

The *Setu* as seen today from Satellite, Courtesy : NASA

The only place to look for evidences around Rama's times, as per the epic Valmiki Ramayana, seems to be the Rama *Setu* or Adam's Bridge.

WHAT TO LOOK FOR?

What does the Ramayana text say about this bridge and what do we find on site?

Contrary to just mentioning in passing, the Ramayana has detailed verses explaining the construction of the bridge. The steps followed by Rama in constructing the bridge seem to be no different from those employed by modern day civil engineering and construction companies.

SURVEY OF THE CONDITIONS

The Ramayana text poetically describes the study of the site conditions by Rama and His team, for a path to cross over to Lanka.

Rama's interaction with the Sea Divinity, *Samudra Deva*

The survey of the conditions of the sea is described as an interaction between Rama and the divinity of the sea, *Samudra Deva.*

> "O, beloved Rama !
> Earth, wind, ether, water and light
> remain fixed in their own nature,
> resorting to their eternal path.
> Therefore,
> I am fathomless and my nature is that
> it is impossible of being swum across.
> It becomes unnatural if I am shallow.
> I am telling you the following device to cross me.
> O, Prince!
> Neither from desire nor ambition
> nor fear, nor from affection,
> I am able to solidify my waters inhabited by Makarah (wild sea creatures).
> O, Rama!
> I shall make it possible to see that you are able to cross over.
> I will arrange a place for the Vanara to cross me
> and bear with it.
> As far as the army crosses me,
> the Makarah will not be aggressive to them.
>
> \- Ramayana 6.22.25 - 28

During this interaction with the sea, they gathered that it was in the nature of these seas to be deep and not shallow, to have waves and fierce sea creatures in them. Given this, it was essential to find a path where Rama and the *Vanara* army would find it easy to cross the sea, which they did. This again has been poetically described as the Sea Divinity, *Samudra Deva,* yielding to Rama and showing Him the path from where, it would be easiest, to cross over.

Planning and Design

Nala, who till then had been a part of the *Vanara* army introduces himself to Rama, presents his credentials and asks for permission to build this bridge over the seas as he has the technical capabilities to do so.

Nala, introduces himself as the biological descendant of Vishwakarma, an architect par excellence and offers his services for the design and construction of a bridge.

"I am a son born of Vishwakarma. I am equal to Vishwakarma. This divinity of Ocean has reminded me. The great ocean spoke the truth. Being unasked, I have not told you my details earlier. I am capable of constructing a bridge across the ocean. Hence, let the foremost of Vanara build the bridge now itself."

Nala, a Vishwakarma, an Engineer

Execution

On the advice of Nala, the *Vanara* then piled different varieties of trees and then large boulders followed by smaller stones to create a causeway over the sea in 5 days, over which they crossed and reached Lanka.

Construction of the bridge

The detailed description of the construction is given in the Ramayana.

"Then, being sent by Rama, hundreds and thousands of Vanara, heroes jumped in joy on all sides, towards the great forest. Those army-chiefs of Vanara, who resembled mountains, broke the rocks and trees there and dragged them away towards the sea. Those Vanara filled the ocean with all types of trees like Sala, Asvakarna, Dhava, bamboo, Kutaja, Arjuna, palmyra, Tilaka, Tinisa, Bilva, Saptaparna, Karnika, in bloom as also mango and Asoka.

The excellent Vanara, the forest animals lifted and brought, like Indra's flag post, some trees with roots intact and some others without roots. From here and there the Vanara brought Palmyra trees, pomegranate shrubs, coconut and Vibhitaka, Karira, Bakula and neem trees. The huge bodied Vanara with mighty strength uprooted elephant-sized rocks and mountains and transported them by mechanical contrivances. The water, raised up due to sudden throwing of mountains in the sea, soured upward towards the sky and from there again, gushed back.

The rocks befalling on all sides perturbed the ocean. Some others drew up strings a hundred Yojana long, - in order to keep the rocks in a straight line. Nala on his part initiated a monumental bridge in the middle of the ocean. The bridge was built at that time with the cooperation of other Vanara, of terrible doings. Some Vanara were holding poles for measuring the bridge and some others collected the materials. Reeds and logs resembling clouds and mountains, brought by hundreds of Vanara, lead by the command of Rama, fastened some parts of the bridge.

Vanara constructed the bridge with trees having blossom at the end of their boughs. Some Vanara looking like demons seized rocks resembling mountains and peaks of mountains and appeared running hither and thither. Then, a tumultuous sound occurred when the rocks were thrown into the sea and when mountains were caused to fall there.

Such was the speed of the Vanara effort, that they built the bridge in just 5 days.

They were possessed of their mission. An army at war does the impossible things, which make it win the war.

On the 1st day, 14 Yojana of bridge were constructed by the Vanara very fast, thrilled with delight as they were, resembling elephants.

In the same manner, on the 2nd day 20 Yojana of bridge were constructed speedily by the Vanara of terrific bodies and of mighty strength.

Thus, on the 3rd day 21 Yojana of the bridge were constructed in the ocean speedily by the Vanara with their colossal bodies.

On the 4th day, a further of 22 Yojána were constructed by the dashing Vanara with a great speed.

In that manner, on the 5th day, the Vanara working quickly constructed 23 Yojana of the bridge up to the other seashore.

That Nala, the strong and illustrious son of Visvakarma and an excellent Vanara built the bridge across the sea as truly as his father would have built it. That beautiful and lovely bridge constructed by Nala across the ocean the abode of crocodiles, shone brightly like a milky way of stars in the sky."

- Yudha Kandam. Sloka 6.22.50 - 72

Bridge Construction - An English Translation

It is pertinent to point out here, the usage of the term, *"mechanical contrivances"* in the poetry. The word used in the original literature is *Yantraha,* meaning mechanical devices. From this description, it is evident that mechanical devices were used then by the *Vanara* to transport huge boulders and trees.

Thus, after surveying the sea and identifying a natural and undulating outcrop from the seabed, on Nala's advice, the *Vanara,* leveraged the outcrop and piled on it, different varieties of trees, some in bloom during that period, to create a wood cushion and then large boulders followed by smaller stones to create a causeway over the sea in 5 days, over which they crossed and reached Lanka.

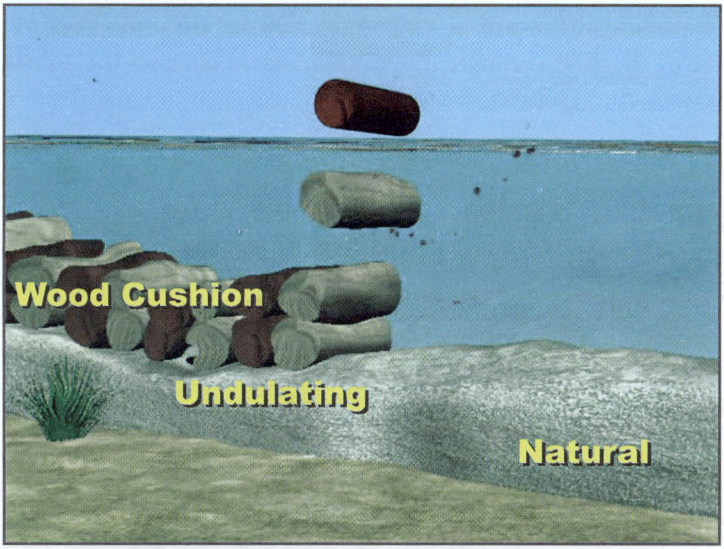

Bridge Construction – A graphical representation
Wood cushion over a natural sea ridge

AND WHAT DO WE SEE?

There is a natural, undulating, underwater sea ridge that rises from the seabed linking the land masses of India and Sri Lanka. This natural formation presented a good foundation over which, the *Vanara* built a causeway bridge.

This would vindicate the interaction between Rama and *Samudra Deva,* the sea, for locating a place in the sea where it would be easy for Rama and His army to cross over.

It is to be noted that, there are claims by some that the Adam's Bridge is a natural formation.

As per the textual statement and its consequent local history over millennia, the bridge was man made.

This has led to a black or white debate of whether the entire structure in the sea which forms the causeway is fully man made or whether it is fully a natural formation.

If the present structure is explored scientifically along its vertical section by digging through the layers of sand bars on the side and if this reveals the layers to be starting with

- the sea bed at the base
- natural rocky outcrop on top of it
- remnants of the tree logs as described in the text on top of the rocky outcrop
- large boulders on top of the logs
- smaller stones on top of the large boulders
- sand on top of the smaller stones,

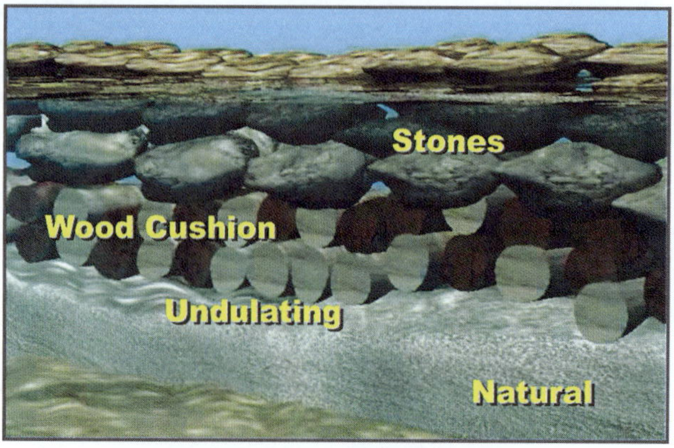

Cross section of bridge detail

then, it would prove that the textual information found in the Ramayana, tallies with the site conditions.

It would reveal that as per the description in the text, it must be **"a man made accretion over a natural sea ridge".**

i.e., **it is most likely a man made bridge constructed over a natural outcrop from the seabed.**

STORY ACROSS AGES - FOR ALL AGES

This description of the construction of the bridge has been common knowledge amongst the people over the times and has found mention in literature of the various periods including the Mahabharatha.

Even in the 20th century, **"Amar Chitra Katha",** an Indian comic series since the 1970s revived the Indian texts and legends in the form of illustrated comics for an interesting and easy read. It is widely accepted as an authentic expression of Indian legends and is very popular among the masses in India, especially the current generation of middle aged, who have grown up reading these. It has influenced many a minds in India and has served as a vital link to keep these legends alive in the minds of the people.

Amar Chitra Katha depiction of wood being used in bridge construction

In their depiction of Ramayana too, they clearly show the layers of the bridge construction, with a wood base, on top of which, large boulders were piled on.

THE MOOT POINT

The question now is, whether, under the layers of, centuries of, hardened sands, do there exist, layers of this bridge, showing remnants of the trees and rocks as placed there by the *Vanara*, as described in the text?

Dr. S. Badrinarayanan, Geologist - former Director of Geological Survey of India and Consultant at the National Institute of Oceanic Technology (NIOT), has done extensive geological research of the bridge and this is what he has to say:

"Geological and geophysical studies of Ram Setu reveal the presence of loose marine sand below the coral layer, clearly indicating that the coral layer in the form of boulders are not natural and formed there on their own, but have been transported by somebody and dumped there; thus clearly establishing the fact that Ram Setu is very much man made in the hoary past."

The use of corals in bridge construction

Corals usually grow on hard rock and closer to the surface of the sea where they can receive sunlight. In the case of the Rama *Setu*, what has been found is that, beneath the corals, there is loose sand. Thus these set of Corals on the *Setu*, could not have grown there on their own, but should have been transported from elsewhere and deposited there.

Since they have been deposited in such a linear manner, in layers of smaller corals on larger corals and given that we have the story in the text talking of the same, we see a convergence between the literary information and the ground reality on the sea bed.

A PERFECT MATCH

The Ramayana text states that the bridge, when it was constructed was 100 *Yojana* in length and the breadth was 10 *Yojana*, making it a ratio of 10:1.

Today, in the same ratio of 10:1 as mentioned in the texts, the bridge from Dhanushkodi in India to Talaimannar in Sri Lanka, measures approx 35 km in length and 3.5 km in breadth, as is the naturally available sea ridge, the base beneath, on which it was built as an accretion.

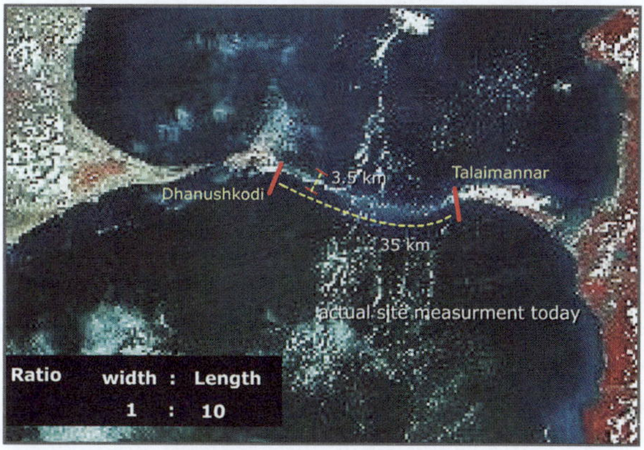

Dimensions of the Bridge

The similarity of the ratio is amazing and serves as a point to prove that this is the same bridge as mentioned in the Ramayana legend.

CAN IT BE FOR REAL?

Could such a bridge really have been built?

From the textual description, what comes out clear is that, there was no structure already jutting over water then (natural or man made) using which they could cross over to Lanka.

What is the opinion of marine archaeologists?

The pioneer in marine archaeology in India, is Dr. S.R. Rao, who undertook marine archaeological expeditions in 1980, to successfully identify the submerged city of Dwaraka, off Saurashtra in the west coast of India.

Dr. S.R.Rao

Former Advisor, Marine Archaeology Centre
National Institute of Oceanography, Goa

In his considered opinion, a man made bridge across the seas would have been possible then because,

"This natural rock connecting the Mannar Island with Rameswaram island is now submerged in the sea owing to the rise in sea level during the last 4000 years or more, but then, it was perhaps in the Intertidal zone and likely to have been further raised by piling up of rubble to enable Rama's followers to reach Lanka.

We found at Dwaraka, a natural rock was dressed suitably as a wharf for berthing ships about 5000 years ago. Similarly the natural rock, in Adam's bridge, connecting Mannar and Rameswaram, must have been used by piling up rubble manually on it, to enable the Vanaras to reach Lanka. For the ancient marine engineers who could build a tidal dock at Lothal in 2300 B.C and modify a ridge for berthing ships at Dwaraka, the piling up of stones on the so called Adam's bridge for an army to reach Lanka was an easy task."

Tracing Archaeological Remains Through The Times

Today, we have very few monuments left behind of Rama's times, that could be taken up for further archaeological studies, to help us to understand this history and the historical personages of those times. Ayodhya and Nala *Setu* are two sites widely believed even today, to bear physical remnants from Ramayana times.

THE CITY OF AYODHYA

Ayodhya was the capital of the kingdom of Rama and his ancestors. It is also the birthplace of Rama. Ayodhya has had a continuity of civilization and people living there and the name of the city along with the tradition of it having been a palace city, has survived till this day.

Archaeological excavations in Ayodhya are on and there have been many interesting finds.

However the lack of any physical archaeological remains dating beyond 3000 to 4000 years ago, at the site claimed to be the birthplace of Rama in Ayodhya, has therefore raised much speculation about the significance and historicity of this place as Rama's birthplace and also about the historicity of Rama too.

Ayodhya is a vast topic by itself, deserving a separate discussion, in a much broader light. Hence, we have examined Ayodhya and its history, using a wholistic approach, in our separate title, **"Ayodhya – War and Peace".**

THE NALA *SETU*

Across times, we find many records of the Nala *Setu* or Rama *Setu*, the bridge built by Rama and the *Vanara* to cross over the sea to Lanka from India.

During the Ramayana Period

After the victorious battle with Ravana, while flying, en route from Lanka to Ayodhya in the *Pushpaka Vimana*, Rama tells Sita,

The Return to Ayodhya in *Pushpaka Vimana*

"Survey the city of Lanka perched on a summit of the Trikuta Mountain, resembling a peak of Mountain Kailasha."

"Here see the landing place on the seashore where having crossed the ocean, we spent that night."

"Here is the bridge called Nala Setu so called because it was constructed by the Vanara Chief Nala, which was so difficult to execute for others."

It is very clear from the above statement that Rama has himself called this bridge *"Nala Setu"* because of the singular effort of Nala in executing this civil engineering marvel.

During The Mahabharatha Period

In the other historical epic of India, the Mahabharatha, Nala *Setu* is described as a protected monument during Mahabharatha times.

Nala Setur iti khyato yo 'dyapi prathito bhuvi ramasyajnac purask - tya dharyate girisacnibha.

"...which even today, popular on earth as Nala's bridge, mountain like, is sustained out of respect for Lord Rama's command."

- Mahabharatha 3.267.45

Further, in the Mahabharatha text, when the 5 *Pandava* brothers roam the forest during their exile period, they visit the *Ashrama* of *Rishi* Markendeya, who regales them with the histories of their land. One such story is that of the Nala *Setu*.

***Rishi* Markendeya narrating stories to *the Pandava* brothers**

Account of the construction of Nala Setu in Mahabharata

...And that mighty army, protected by Nala and Nila and Angada and Kratha and Mainda and Dwivida, marched forth for achieving the purpose of Raghava. And encamping successively, without interruption of any kind, on wide and healthy tracts and valleys abounding with fruits and roots and water and honey and meat, the Vanara at last reached the shores of the briny sea. And like unto a second ocean, that mighty army with its countless colours, having reached the shores of the sea, took up its abode there. Then the illustrious son of Dasaratha, addressing Sugreeva amongst all those foremost Vanara, spoke unto him these words that were suited to the occasion, 'This army is large. The ocean also is difficult to cross. What way, therefore, commends itself to thee for crossing the ocean?'

At these words, many vain-glorious Vanara answered, 'We are fully able to cross the sea. ' This answer, however, was not of much use, as all could not avail of its meaning. Then, some of the Vanara proposed to cross the sea in boats, and some in rafts of various kinds. Rama, however, conciliating them all, said, 'This cannot be. 'The sea here is a full hundred Yojanas in width. All the Vanara, ye heroes, will not be able to cross it. This proposal, therefore, that ye have made, is not consonant to reason. Besides we have not the number of boats necessary for carrying all our troops. How, again, can one like us raise such obstacles in the way of the merchants? Our army is very large. The foe wilt make a great havoc if a hole is detected. Therefore, to cross the sea in boats and rafts doth not recommend itself to me. I will, however, pray to the Ocean for the necessary means. Foregoing food, I will lie down on the shore. He will certainly show himself to me. If, however, he doth not show himself, I will chastise him then by means of my great weapons that are more blazing than fire itself and are incapable of being baffled!'

Having said these words, both Rama and Lakshmana touched water and duly laid themselves down on a bed of kusa grass on the seashore. The divine and illustrious Ocean, that lord of male and female rivers surrounded by aquatic animals, then appeared unto Rama in a vision. And addressing Rama in sweet accents, the genius of the Ocean, surrounded by countless mines of gems, said, 'O son of Kausalya, tell me what aid, O bull among men, I am to render thee! I also have sprung from the race of Ikshwaku and am, therefore, a relative of thine!' Rama replied unto him, saying, 'O lord of rivers, male and female, I desire thee to grant me a way for my troops, passing along which I may slay the Ten-headed (Ravana), that wretch of Pulastya's race! If thou dost not grant the way I beg of thee, I will then dry thee up by means of my celestial arrows inspired with mantras!'

And hearing these words of Rama, the genius of Varuna abode, joining his hands, answered in great affliction, 'I do not desire to put any obstacle in thy way. I am no foe of thine! Listen, O Rama, to these words, and having listened, do what is proper! If, at thy command, I get a way for the passage of thy army, others then, from strength of their bows, will command me to do the same! In thy army there is a Vanara of the name of Nala, who is a skilled engineer. And endued with great strength, Nala is the son of Tashtri, the divine artificer of the Universe. And whether it is wood, or grass or stone, that he will throw into my waters, I will support the same on my seabed, and thus wilt thou have a bridge over me, through which to reach Lanka!'

And having said these words, the genius of the Ocean disappeared. And Rama awaking, called Nala unto him and said, 'Build thou a bridge over the sea! Thou alone, I am sure, art able to do it!' And it was by this means that the descendant of Kakutstha's race caused a bridge to be built that was 10 Yojana in width and a 100 Yojana in length. And to this day that bridge is celebrated over all the world by the name of Nala's bridge.

Mahabharata, Vanaparva, Ramopakhyanam

An English Translation of the relevant passage from Mahabaratha

In the Mahabharatha text, the Nala *Setu* is not only discussed as an old story, but the *Setu* is also used by one of the characters of the Mahabharatha period to walk over to Lanka.

Sahadeva, one of the *Pandava* brothers, during his exile wished to see the marvel of Nala *Setu* and travelled down south to the Nala *Setu* to view it, to be amazed by it and also to offer his respects to this engineering marvel.

The *Pandava,* Bheema's son Ghatothkacha, also travelled down south along with Sahadeva, his paternal uncle. Ghatothkacha was a *Rakshasa* by birth, from his maternal lineage. So, while Sahadeva stayed back on the Indian side of the Nala *Setu,* Ghatothkacha walked over the Nala *Setu,* into Lanka, to meet the descendants of Vibhishana – the King of Lanka, also of the *Rakshasa* clan, the clan to which Ghatothkacha himself belonged.

Sahadeva

Ghatothkacha

Vibhishana's descendants in Lanka

These references in the Mahabharatha tell us a few things

- The events of Mahabharatha happened well after the events of Ramayana
- The Nala *Setu* was venerated as a civil engineering marvel even during the Mahabharatha period, i.e., 2000 years after its construction
- The Nala *Setu* was a protected monument of their times i.e., 3000 BCE
- The reason for construction and the details of civil engineering were part of the celebrated folklore of the land which is evident from the story told by *Rishi* Markandeya
- People from all over India, such as Sahadeva, visited the Nala *Setu* to see the engineering marvel
- Ghatothkacha of the *Rakshasa* clan too walked over the Nala *Setu* to meet his *Rakshasa* clan members. This shows the brotherhood among people across the lands.

Till 600 years ago

If this was a continuously used foot bridge to walk across between India and Lanka, for more than a couple of thousands of years, when it did it cease to be used as a foot bridge?

This Nala *Setu,* even though built in such a short time, 7200 years ago, was so well engineered and constructed, that it lasted for the next 6400 years. In the year 1480 CE, there was a major storm, probably like a modern day like Tsunami, which washed away portions of the bridge. The remains became a dilapidated structure and hence became unusable.

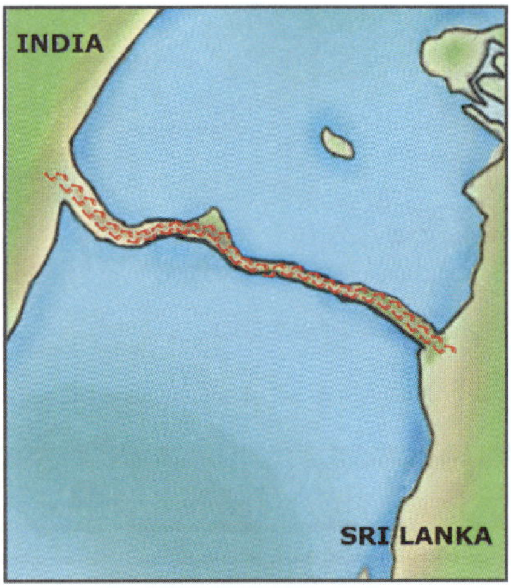

Foot traffic across the *Setu* till 1480 CE

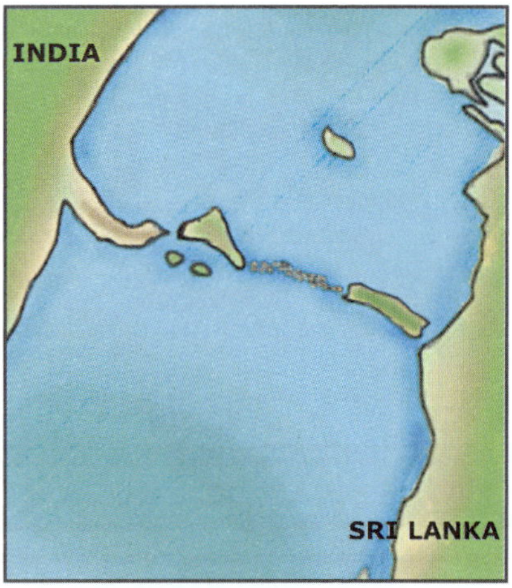

The disjointed and dilapidated *Setu* post the 1480 CE storm

This fact is recorded in the Manual of Madras Presidency written by C.D. Maclean in 1902, and has been reproduced in the Tamil Nadu Gazette too.

Summing up

Thus the *Setu* has been discussed in literature as a protected monument through the ages.

The findings at the site of the Rama *Setu* tally with the literature on the construction of the bridge.

The *Setu* can be dated using an integrated approach, to about 7000 years ago, which will make it one of the oldest known structures of the world.

The detailed reports of the few surveys conducted till date, point to the *Setu* being a man made accretion over a natural sea ridge.

Throughout history, there have been repeated references to this bridge and Rama as a historical personage, in various places and forms. These continuous references provide credible inputs on the historicity of Rama, the existence of the bridge and its usage through the ages.

INSCRIPTIONS

Rajendra Chola

Rajendra Chola I, ruled from Thanjavur in South India, between 1018-1048 CE. During his rule, he had his deeds inscribed on copper plates which are now known as "Tiruvalangadu plates".

On one such plate, in verse no.80, he inscribes about *"Rama building a bridge over the seas"*.

A painting of Rajendra Chola

Tiruvalangadu Plates

(V. 80.) The lord of the **R â g h a v a s** (*i.e.*, Râma) constructing a bridge across the water of the ocean with (*the assistance of*) able monkeys, killed with great difficulty the king of **L a ṅ k â** (*i.e.*, Râvana) with sharp-edged arrows; (*but*), this terrible General of that (*king* Aruṇmoḻivarman) crossed the ocean by ships and burnt the Lord of Laṅkâ (Ceylon). Hence **R â m a** is (*surely*) surpassed by this (Chôḻa General).

The lord of the Raghava (i.e., Rama)

constructing a bridge across the water of the ocean

with (the assistance of) ***vanara***.

killed with great difficulty the king of Lanka

(i.e., Ravana) ***with sharp-edged arrows***;

this terrible General of that (king Arunmolivarman)

crossed the ocean by ships

and burnt the Lord of Lanka.

Hence Rama is surpassed by this (Chola General).

Tiruvalangadu Plates English Translation

Krishnadevaraya

Krishnadevaraya was one of the celebrated medieval kings of India who ruled over the Vijayanagara empire from Hampi in present day Karnataka state.

Krishna Raya

Virupaksha temple

Stone Chariot - Vithala Temple

Narasimha Shrine

Remains from the Vijayanagar Empire, Hampi

In his inscriptions over 500 years ago, he describes about this bridge Rama *Setu;* the relevant inscriptions being Inscription dated Saka 1430 (1508 CE) available in Epigraphia Indica Volume 1 1892, Pg. 363 – 366.

The following three verses have been taken from Epigraphia Indica Volume 1 1892.

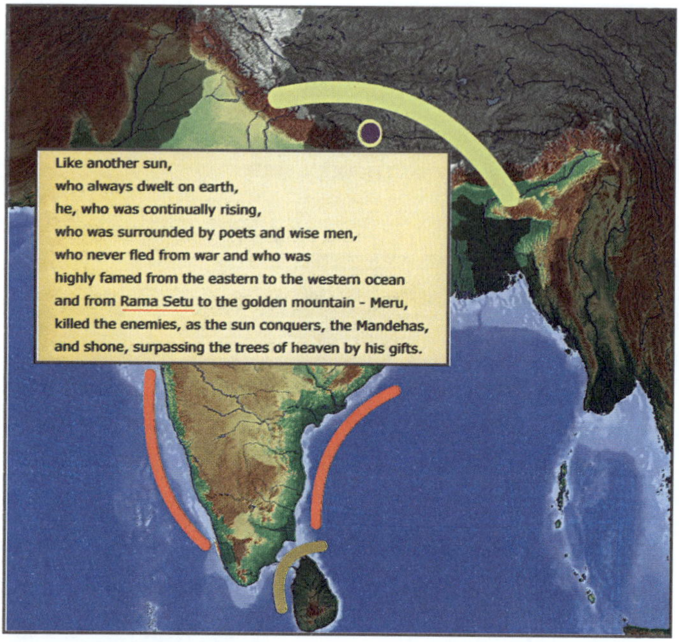

Verse - 8

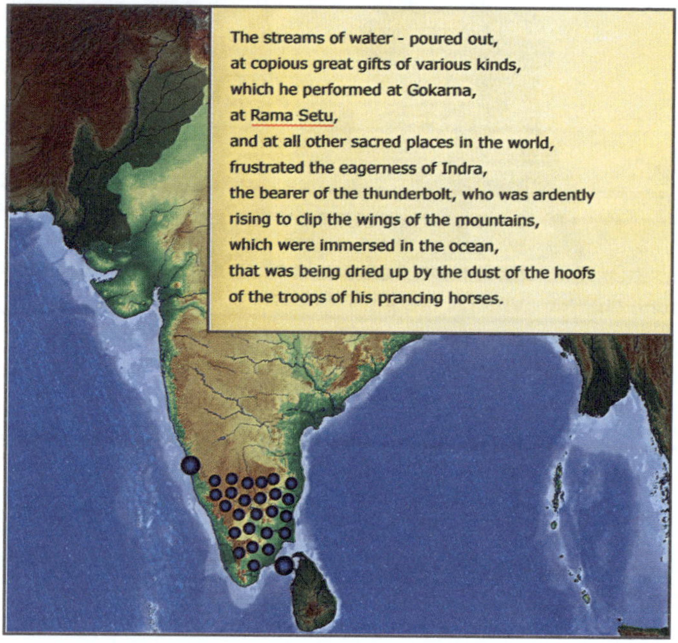

Verse - 17

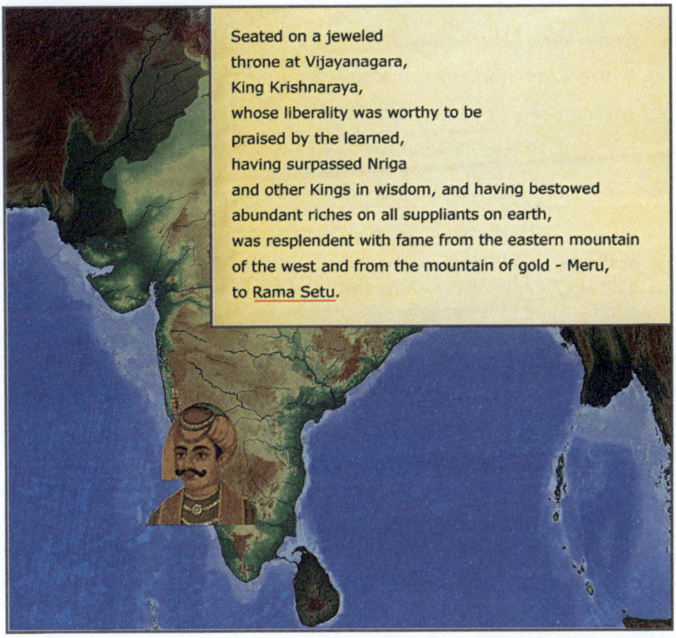

Verse - 29

COINS

The coins of India, especially of south India and those of Sri Lanka, repeatedly mention the *Setu* as a landmark and popular symbol.

The Parantaka Chola Coins

Parantaka Chola, one of the Chola kings of 907 CE, then issued coins of his valour, wherein for reference he mentions the bridge built by the *Vanara Sena.*

Coins with Samskrt text in Grantha script

ramie sriramatirthe kavivara nikaraih baddhaSetu prabandhe kanyatirthe jitanamadaritamapi dis'e mandane dakshinasyaah srirange cahis'alyas'ayitamurabhidi s'yamapogabhirame hemnaviryancitena kshitipatikarot yastulabharakarma

"This ruler performed tulabhara with gold acquired by his valour, at the beautiful Sriramatirtha, where the ablest of Vanara flocks built the bridge; at the Kanyaatirtha which subdued the southern quarters and at Srirangam, beautiful by the areca groves, where Sri Vishnu reclines on his serpent couch."

\- Sriramatirtha

Sriraamatirtha in this text refers to Rameswaram and *Kanyatirtha* refers to Kanyakumari, the southern tip of India.

Setupati coins

Raja Setupati

The kings of Ramanathapuram, where the *Setu* is, have been traditionally known by the title *'Setupati'*, meaning the "Guardians of the Bridge". These kings regularly minted coins with the term *'Setu'* mentioned on one side of the coin.

From the series of these coins, we can see that it was not a one off practice, but a continuity of tradition over the centuries. The kings of Ramanathapuram, the *Setupati* Raja took their role seriously of guarding this bridge with their kinship.

Obverse : Sri Ganapati, seated

Reverse : in Tamil, *'Se-Tu-Pa-Ti'*

Sri Lankan Coins

On the Sri Lankan side, The *Yazhpanam Arya Chakravarti,* kings of Jaffna, who ruled between 1284 and 1597 CE issued a series of coins with the word *Setu* mentioned on it, indicating that they were the guardians of the bridge from the Lankan side.

Obverse : Standing king with Lamp, Reverse : Seated king, Tamil legend *Setu*

Obverse : Standing king with crown, Reverse : Bull, *Setu*

The rulers of Nallur near Jaffna, in Sri Lanka, who ruled between 13th and 17th century also issued coins with the word *Setu* inscribed on it indicating that they were also the guardians of the *Setu.*

Coins showing Nandi and a peacock with word *Setu* appearing below

This continuity of tradition has been bought forth by the researcher of Jaffna, Prof.S.Pathamanathan in his article on Coins titled *"Yaalpana Iraachchiyam"* in the year 1992.

" நாணயங்களிலே வரும் சேது எனும் மொழி சேதுகாவலன் என்ற விருதின் சுருக்கமே எனச் சிந்திக்கலாம். "i.e. "The word Sētu in the coins could be considered as the shortened fom of the epithet Sētukāvalan."

TRAVELOGUES

Many travellers over the past thousand years who have passed by the *Setu,* have recorded the details of this bridge, its antiquity, its usage, construction, nature and origin. This continuity of the travellers' notes over a thousand year period, brings forth to us that the name, the knowledge and the usage of the bridge is not a new fad, but is a continuous knowledge of the locals of that land.

Al-Biruni describing Geography of India

Al-Biruni 1030 CE

"Next to a great bay in which Singaldib lies, i.e., the island Sarandib (Ceylon).

On the coast is Ummalnara, then Ramsher (Rameshwar) *opposite Sarandib; the distance of the sea between them is 12 farsakh.*

Between Ramsher and Setubandha 2 farsakh. Setubandha means bridge of the ocean. It is the dike of Rama, the son of Dasaratha which he built from the continent to the castle Lanka. At present it consists of isolated mountains between which the ocean flows.

Sixteen farsakh from Setubandha towards the east is Kihkind. The mountains of the Vanara."

Kitabu'l Hind

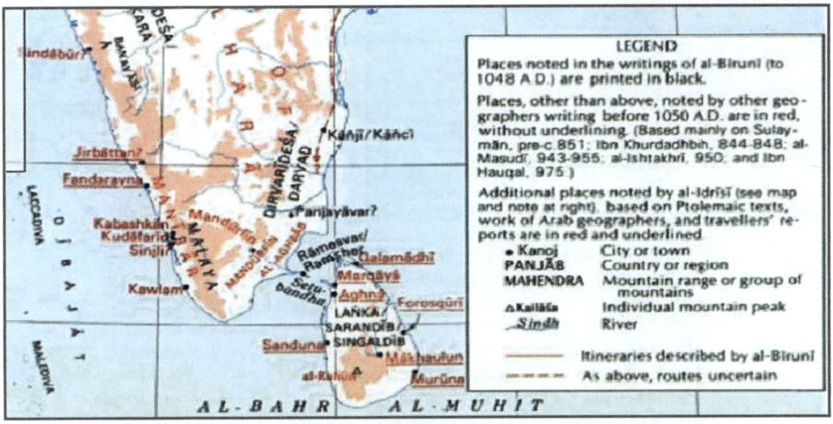

Map of South India based on Al-Biruni's description now at Chicago Library

Marco Polo of Venice

Marco Polo of Venice, who travelled between the years 1271 – 1295, was one of the earliest European travellers to India.

Marco Polo

He travelled over much of China, South East Asia and on his return leg, sailed past the Rama *Setu* before stopping in the Malabar coast. He mentions Rama *Setu* and its usage in his travelogue.

Marco Polo's Travelogue

[3] The name of this country, which both in the Bâsle edition and the older Latin is Maabar, and Moabar in the epitomes, is Malabar in the text of Ramusio, of which the former has been supposed a corruption; but the reverse is the case, for circumstances unequivocally point to the southern part of the coast of Coromandel as the place where the fleet arrived after leaving Ceylon; and what puts the matter beyond all doubt is, that the province of Malabar is afterwards distinctly mentioned in its proper place. Maàbar, signifying a "passage, ferry, ford, trajectus" (see the dictionaries of Meninski and Richardson), was an appellation given by the Mahometans to what we call the Tinevelly, Madura, and, perhaps, Tanjore countries—from their vicinity, as it would seem, to the celebrated chain of sand-banks and coral reefs named Rama's or Adam's bridge. It is has now fallen into disuse, but is to be found in the works of all the oriental geographers and historians who have treated of this portion of India.

H. G. Bohn, Translation of Marsden revised
Page 380, foot note 3

Marco Polo mentions Malabar Wealth and Rama's bridge *Setu Bandh.*

Varthema

Ludovico de Varthema, an Italian traveller, travelled extensively over Egypt, Syria, Arabia, Persia and India. He also travelled to the Rama *Setu* and mentions it in his book.

I am surprised that Dr. Vincent, who was well acquainted with Ramusio's Collection, has made no reference to this *Cael* or *Coil* in his identification of the *Kolkhi* of the author of the *Periplus* with the *Kôru* and *Calligicum* of Ptolemy and the *Kôlis* of Dionysius, as the existence of a town of that name, and in the locality occupied by *Cael*, seems to supply the only desideratum for removing the doubt which attaches to his deductions. I quote his argument in full, leaving the reader to form his own judgment on my suggestion :—" Ptolemy has still another particular which is very remarkable; for as he places the northern point of his Taprôbane opposite to a promontory named Kôru, so he has an island Kôru between the two, and a Tala-Côri on Ceylon; and Kôry, he says, is the same as Calligicum...The expedition of Ram to Ceylon, and his victory over Rhavan or Rhaban, king of that island, is one of the wildest fables of Hindoo mythology, but he passed into the island at the strait, since called, by the Mohamedans, Adam's Bridge. The whole country round, in consequence of this, preserves the memorial of his conquest. There is a Ramanad-buram on the continent close to the bridge; a Rami-Ceram, or country of Ram, the island close to the continent; [*Rameswaram*, called *Rammanana Kojel* by Baldæus, and *Ramonan Coil* by D'Anville ;] and a Point Rama on the continent. The bridge itself, formed by the shoals between Rami-ceram and Manaar, is Rama's Bridge; and in Rami-ceram is Raman-Koil, the temple of Ram. This Koil or temple [*Koil* means a temple in Malayalim] is undoubtedly the origin of Kôru; and the repetition of it three times in Ptolemy is in perfect correspondence with the various allusions to Ram at the present

The Travels of Ludovico di Varthema in Egypt, Syria, Arabia Deserta and Arabia Felix, in Persia, India
George Percy Badger, John Winter Jones, 1863, Published for the Hakluyt Society, Translated from the original Italian edition. Page. 185

Ludovico de Varthema, 1470–1517

The Travels of Ludovico de Varthema

Asiatic Society, 1799

The Royal Asiatic society was started in Bengal by the Europeans who had settled in India, to do research on Indian Knowledge. In their research papers they also speak about this bridge having been built there based on their research and recordings. Few of the examples being, references to the bridge called *Setband,* broken in 3 places.

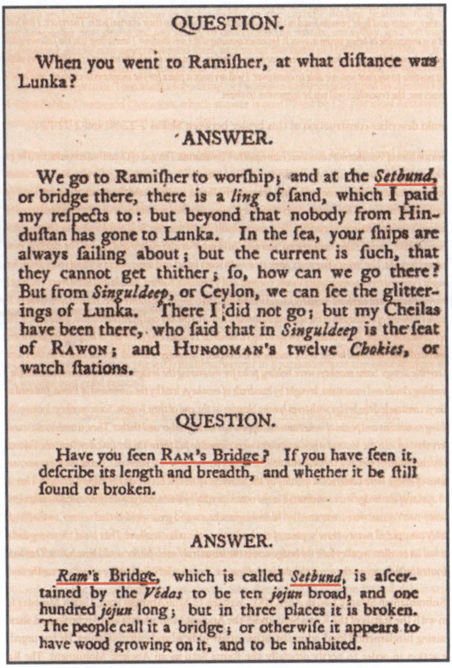

QUESTION.

When you went to Ramiſher, at what diſtance was Lunka?

ANSWER.

We go to Ramiſher to worſhip; and at the *Setbund,* or bridge there, there is a *ling* of ſand, which I paid my reſpects to: but beyond that nobody from Hinduſtan has gone to Lunka. In the ſea, your ſhips are always ſailing about; but the current is ſuch, that they cannot get thither; ſo, how can we go there? But from *Singuldeep*, or Ceylon, we can ſee the glitterings of Lunka. There I did not go; but my Cheilas have been there, who ſaid that in *Singuldeep* is the ſeat of RAWON; and HUNOOMAN's twelve *Chokies*, or watch ſtations.

QUESTION.

Have you ſeen RAM's Bridge? If you have ſeen it, deſcribe its length and breadth, and whether it be ſtill ſound or broken.

ANSWER.

Ram's Bridge, which is called *Setbund*, is aſcertained by the *Védas* to be ten *jojun* broad, and one hundred *jojun* long; but in three places it is broken. The people call it a bridge; or otherwiſe it appears to have wood growing on it, and to be inhabited.

Asiatic Researches or Transactions of the Society Instituted in Bengal

"The people call it a bridge; or otherwise it appears to have wood growing on it, and to be inhabited."

The details of this bridge, is in the form of a question answer, in the English of those days, which is an interesting read now. Note the usage of alphabet *'f'* for **'s'** in the printing of those days.

ASSORTED OBSERVATIONS

Various other researchers while working on their respective areas of research, while covering the geography of India and the Southern part of India, have referred to this bridge as Rama's bridge, going to show that this bridge and its association with Rama was popular and had spread far and wide.

The northern parts of Ceylon are chiefly left to the natives; but the town of Jafna, in a detached isle, was a Dutch settlement. The great pearl-fishing is conducted in the gulf of Manár; a miserable place in a sandy district, to which water is brought from Aripoo, a village four miles to the south; the shoals near Rama's bridge supply inexhaustible stores of this valued production.

William Fordyce Mavor 1807, University History Ancient & Modern Oxford University - Page 216

Sir William adds, that the characters called "Nagari," in which the languages of India were originally written, with no greater variation in their forms, by the change of straight lines to curves, or conversely, than the Cufic characters received in their way from Arabia, "are still "adopted in more than twenty-eight kingdoms, from the borders of Cashgar and Khoten, to "Rama's bridge, and from the Sindhi to the river of Siam;" that the square Chaldaic letters in

Rishi **Markendeya narrating stories to** ***the Pandava*** **brothers**

six years before Christ[4]. The particular object of this inscription is to record the liberality of a certain renowned conqueror named Deb Pal Deb, who overran all India, from the sources of the Ganges to Rama's bridge at Ceylon, which is celebrated in the Ramayana.

Arnold Hermann 1833, Historical researches into the politics, intercourse, and trade of the principal nations of antiquity. Translated from the German Oxford University - Page 89

समुद्रार(रः) 1. *m.* A shark, a whale; *Ráma's* bridge. [time.

समुद्रिय (यः-या-यं) *a.* Marine, mari-

William Yates 1846, A Dictionary of Samskrt and English, designed for the use of private students and of Indian colleges and schools, Baptist Mission Press - Page 821

The *characters*, in which the languages of *India* were originally written, are called *Nágarí*, from *Nagara*, a city, with the word *Déva* ſometimes prefixed, becauſe they are believed to have been taught by the Divinity himſelf, who preſcribed the artificial order of them in a voice from heaven. Theſe letters, with no greater variation in their form by the change of ſtraight lines to curves, or converſely, than the *Cusick* alphabet has received in its way to *India*, are ſtill adopted in more than twenty kingdoms and ſtates, from the borders of *Cashgar* and *Khoten*, to *Ráma's* Bridge, and from the *Sindhu* to the river of *Siam*. Nor can I help believing,

Thomas Horsfield 1851, A catalogue of the mammalian in the Museum of the Hon. East India Company, East India Company Museum

Rama and all the allied forces marched down to the Coromandel coast, and making a bridge by casting rocks into the sea passed quickly into Lanka.* Vestiges of Rama's bridge may still be seen, occasioning much inconvenience to navigators, who are obliged to lighten heavy-burdened vessels before they can pass the rocks and sandbanks of the Straits of Manaar. After fighting a few battles, the

Charlotte Speir Manning George Scharf 1856, Life in Ancient India Oxford University - Page 117

Tamil race. The *Vellaler* or agricultural caste comes next, and then the *Maravar* and *Kallar*, or robber castes. The Prince of Ramnad, who is hereditary guardian of Rama's bridge, belongs to the Maravars, and the Rajah of Tondiman to the Kallars. Below the robber castes are the *Shanars* or

About Ramnad King as Guardian of the Bridge Clements Robert Markham 1862, Travels in Peru and India, Murray - Page 423

SATELLITE IMAGERY

NASA through their satellites have been photographing the skies and different parts of the world.

In this process, they have also photographed South India and Sri Lanka. In these satellite images, the bridge is clearly visible as a causeway. NASA in their statement on these photographs has stated that the lands at both ends of the causeway, are over 1.7 million years old and that the causeway connecting these 2 lands also appears to be old and manmade due to its unique curvature.

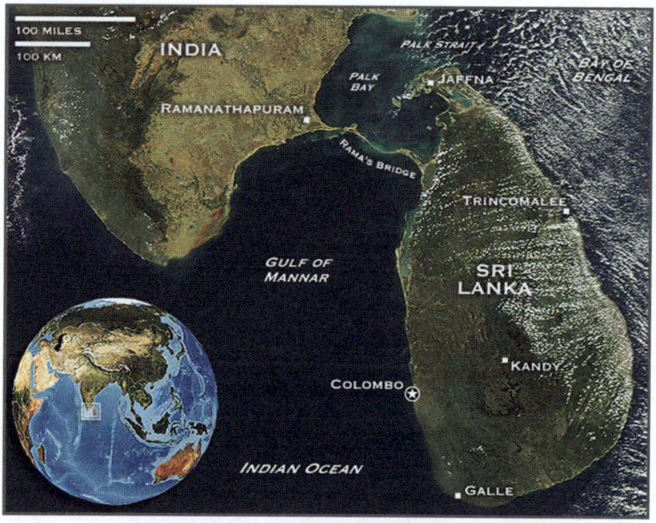

Satellite Image showing the Adam's Bridge

Artificial causeway over a natural formation?

In his book, **"A Concise History of Ceylon",** C. W. Nicholas raises a vital question –

"Did the Pamban passage exist before 1549? Was it an artificial work?"

"A straight rocky barrier, presenting a wall-like appearance on the northern side, sandstone formations consisting of large masses of rock with a flat upper surface, now stretches for about 6,000 feet between the Indian mainland and Pamban island.

Through a 200 feet gap in the great dam runs the Pamban passage. The rocky barrier is a natural and partly artificial causeway over low, sandstone based isthmus."

Similarly, many others have also raised questions on similar lines and brought it out in their respective works such as **"The Masses of Rock"** by Baldaeus, **"The Rows of Cliffs"** by Becker, and **"The Great Dam Modern Charts"**.

A GOVERNOR'S REQUEST

1914

For me Rameshwaram,
very much like India as a whole is the real world
History can be events or memory of events....
Along the Bay of Bengal the Madras Presidency runs,
Rameshwaram adorning its Southern boundaries.
And then Adam's Bridge-
a reef of sunken islands'
beckons us across the Palk Straits to Ceylon,
where civilisation flourished more than 2000 years ago.
All these are a little part of my beloved Presidency .
From early times in India,
it is ethnology, philology, and archaeology
that give and will give us some notions of the truth.
From archaeology much can be expected.
I would earnestly request you to direct
the Archaeological Survey of India (ASI)
to undertake an extensive
and intensive survey of Rameshwaram
and its beautiful environs,
particularly with reference to the historic
and primordial Adam's Bridge.

Lord Pentland
Governor of Madras

Copy to
Sir Alexander Tottenham
District Collector
Ramanathapuram

Lord Pentland

Lord Pentland, Governor of Madras, during the years 1912-1919, as a part of his official tours visited the southern districts. When he happened to camp at Rama *Setu,* he was amazed at the construction and had then written this letter to Lord Hardinge, the then Viceroy of India.

Lord Hardinge

From reading this letter, it is obvious that Lord Pentland was moved by the bridge and then wanted the Archaeological Survey of India to take up its technical survey.

So the call for a technical survey of the bridge in recent times does not seem to be a new request, but is now close to a 100 years old. The call for a technical survey, as evident from Lord Pentland's request, is a call from all those in quest of the truth and in search of their true history. If it is indeed found to be a man made structure, then all can revel in its antiquity and marvel at the ingenuity of mankind along with the flow of time and the turn of events with it.

CONTINUOUS REFERENCES

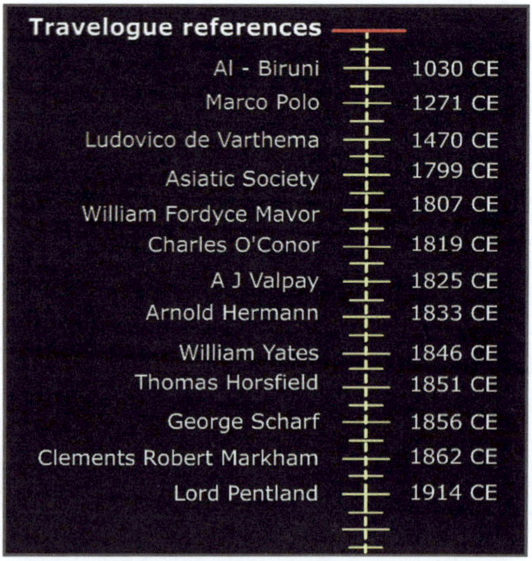

A summary of repeated reference to the Nala *Setu*

We see that, repeatedly over time, across the last 1000 years, we have records of various visitors to this part of the land, which reveal the opinion held forth on the bridge, amongst common men in the society as well as visitors to India. It is interesting to note how this bridge was commonly accepted, in a matter of fact manner, as a bridge built during the times of Rama.

MAPS

When the Europeans came to this side of the globe, they created charts of these areas, in which they have collected information from locals and called this bridge to be *RamaSetu, Setubanda,* Adam's Bridge. Some of the prominent early maps being,

French map of South India showing ports and their controllers Guillaume de Lisle, 1723 Carte des Cotes de Malabar et de Coromandel

Source : David Rumsey collection

Ramancoil - Malabar Bowen Map - Netherlands 1747

Source : David Rumsey collection

James Rennel – Charting the Land

James Rennel was the first Cartographer of India. He was the first Surveyor General of East India Company. As a pioneer in map making, his map of 1st January, 1788 is considered as a valuable, early research material.

Map of Hindoostan

James Rennel Map

James Rennel
1st Surveyor General

In this map, he too describes the bridge area as Raman Coil and Adam's Bridge.

Maps from Ceylon

Similarly the Dutch maps of this region show this bridge as Adam's Brugg.

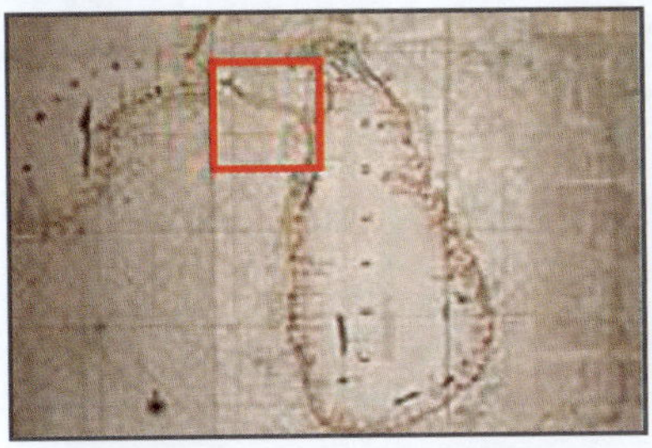

Ceylon - Ceilon Leupe catalogue, 17th century, Netherlands.

Kaart van de zuidelijke punt van Voor-Indië met Ceilon en de Adamsbrug

Copper plate

The Sri Lanka Archaeological Department has old copper plates in which the *Setu*, bridge is clearly shown.

Close up map of bridge

GOVERNMENT RECORDS – FROM THEN TO NOW

Government records are the primary source of information of any land, its structures and their history. In India too, the government records give us repeated information on this bridge. Let us see some of the prominent government records.

The Survey of India

This bridge is recognized as a prominent structure in The Survey Of India.

The Survey of India logo adopted in the year 1767, seen in this image here, has its slogan as *"asethu himachalam"*, meaning "from *Setu* to Himalaya".

Survey of India Logo

Stevens Survey Report

Robert Palk of Government of Madras, in 1763, encouraged his clergyman Lt.William Stevens to survey the Adams Bridge. Stevens extensively surveyed the area and gave it the name "Palk Strait" or "Palk Bay", in honour of his superior.

Stevens in his Survey Report calls this Adams Bridge as "Rama *Setu*" and gives details of its layers. The survey copy is now housed in:

1. Tamil Nadu Archives and
2. Survey of India -Head Quarters in Dehradun

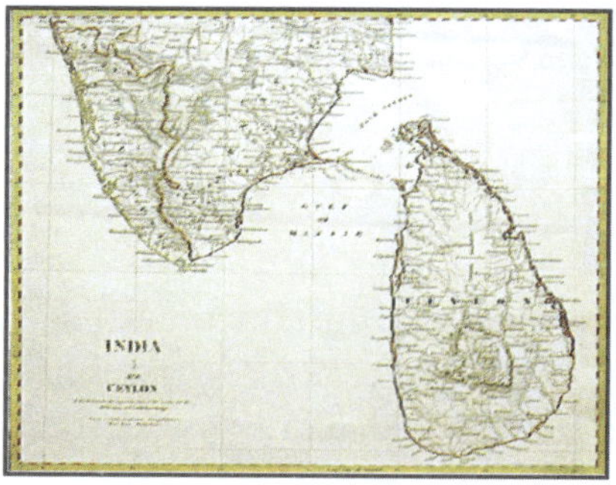

Steven Survey Report Map

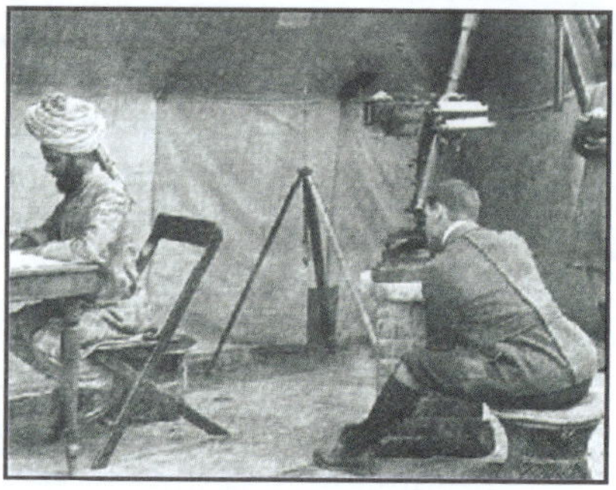

Stevens doing Survey

Imperial Gazetteer of India

Every country has its Gazette regularly prepared by the Government of the time. During the Imperial rule of India by the British an "Imperial Gazette" was prepared. In this Gazette, Adam's Bridge and how it came to be, is described along with how the British planned to construct a Railway line to Ceylon on this dilapidated bridge.

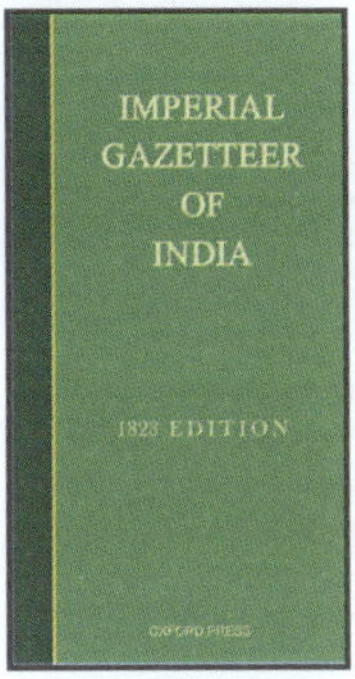

Imperial Gazetteer of India

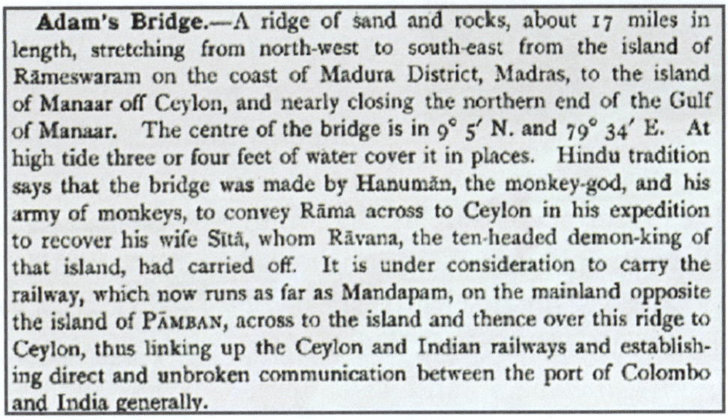

Adam's Bridge.—A ridge of sand and rocks, about 17 miles in length, stretching from north-west to south-east from the island of Rāmeswaram on the coast of Madura District, Madras, to the island of Manaar off Ceylon, and nearly closing the northern end of the Gulf of Manaar. The centre of the bridge is in $9^\circ\ 5'$ N. and $79^\circ\ 34'$ E. At high tide three or four feet of water cover it in places. Hindu tradition says that the bridge was made by Hanumān, the monkey-god, and his army of monkeys, to convey Rāma across to Ceylon in his expedition to recover his wife Sītā, whom Rāvana, the ten-headed demon-king of that island, had carried off. It is under consideration to carry the railway, which now runs as far as Mandapam, on the mainland opposite the island of PĀMBAN, across to the island and thence over this ridge to Ceylon, thus linking up the Ceylon and Indian railways and establishing direct and unbroken communication between the port of Colombo and India generally.

Adam's Bridge Text

CD Maclean Report

During their rule, the British had prepared a Manual of Administration for each of the Presidencies of India. For the Madras Presidency also, a Manual was made by CD Maclean in 1902. In this, he clearly states that this bridge was in continuous use till 1480 CE, when a major storm breached it and since then it ceased to be a foot traffic bridge.

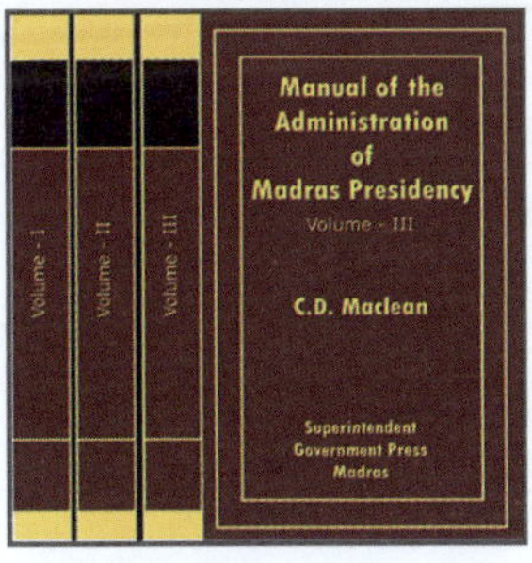

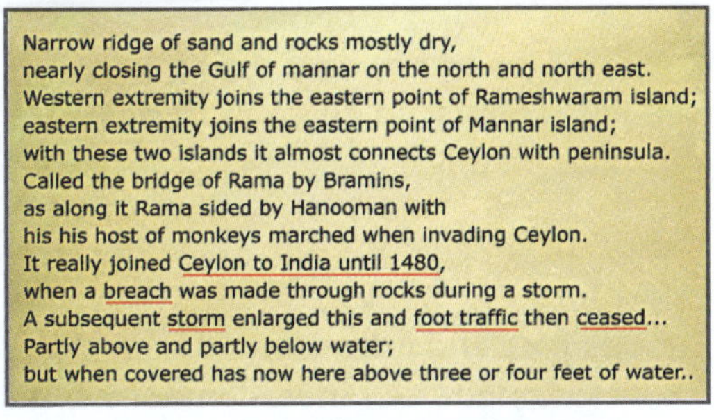

Narrow ridge of sand and rocks mostly dry,
nearly closing the Gulf of mannar on the north and north east.
Western extremity joins the eastern point of Rameshwaram island;
eastern extremity joins the eastern point of Mannar island;
with these two islands it almost connects Ceylon with peninsula.
Called the bridge of Rama by Bramins,
as along it Rama sided by Hanooman with
his his host of monkeys marched when invading Ceylon.
It really joined Ceylon to India until 1480,
when a breach was made through rocks during a storm.
A subsequent storm enlarged this and foot traffic then ceased...
Partly above and partly below water;
but when covered has now here above three or four feet of water..

Text from "Manual of Administration of the Madras Presidency"

Gazetteers

Ramanathapuram District Gazette

The Government of the southern Indian state of Tamil Nadu, has been regularly preparing the Gazetteer of the state and its districts.

The information given in the Gazetteer is considered to be authentic and reliable, compiled as an encyclopaedic reference material for researchers as declared and signed by none less than the Chief Minister of the state in the foreword to the Gazetteer.

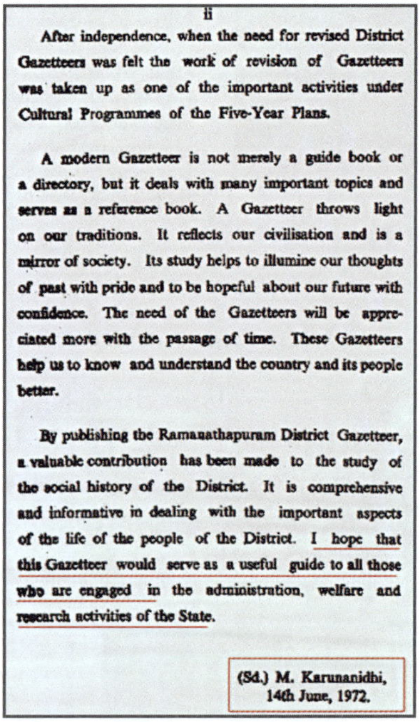

ii

After independence, when the need for revised District Gazetteers was felt the work of revision of Gazetteers was taken up as one of the important activities under Cultural Programmes of the Five-Year Plans.

A modern Gazetteer is not merely a guide book or a directory, but it deals with many important topics and serves as a reference book. A Gazetteer throws light on our traditions. It reflects our civilisation and is a mirror of society. Its study helps to illumine our thoughts of past with pride and to be hopeful about our future with confidence. The need of the Gazetteers will be appreciated more with the passage of time. These Gazetteers help us to know and understand the country and its people better.

By publishing the Ramanathapuram District Gazetteer, a valuable contribution has been made to the study of the social history of the District. It is comprehensive and informative in dealing with the important aspects of the life of the people of the District. I hope that this Gazetteer would serve as a useful guide to all those who are engaged in the administration, welfare and research activities of the State.

(Sd.) M. Karunanidhi,
14th June, 1972.

The foreword to the Gazetteer

The Gazetteer of Ramanathapuram District, published in the year 1972, goes on to clearly speak of the "Adam's Bridge" as *"Setu Palam"* and *"Rama Setu"* and calls it as *"tiruvanai"* meaning a Sacred Dam in Tamil.

It also states that this is also called the *"Ramar Palam"* because it was built by the *"Kuranguppadai"* or *"Vanara Sena"*, the army of *Vanara* and it was in use till 1480 A.D, when it was washed away in a storm.

Vanara is loosely translated by many, as monkeys but we shall see in detail as to who these *Vanara* were, later in this book.

These statements in the Gazette, clearly bring forth, that the Government of the land, through the hands of the then Chief Minister, had accepted and acknowledged the tradition, that this bridge, as per the local legends, was indeed built by the *"Vanara Sena"*.

21

Off shore Dangers of the Rameswaram Island.

Rocks awash lie about 1½ miles eastward of the north-eastern end of the Rameswaram Island and shoal water extends about a mile outside them. In this vicinity, the depths should not be shoaled to less than a depth of 5 fathoms. Devil's point or *Pishasu Munai* ([illegible]) is situated 7 miles east-northeast from Pamban and 32 miles east of Ramanathapuram at Latitude 9° 19'38·12" N. and Longitude 79° 21' 11·49" E. All boats and ships will have to avoid this shoal of 5' high by going away from the Point.

Gulf of Manar:—The Gulf of Manar is the portion of the Indian Ocean lying between the western coast of Ceylon and the eastern coast of the Madras State. Its northern limit is the chain of islets and rocks called Adam's Bridge which extends from the western extreme of the Manar Island at the north-eastern end of the Gulf for about 16 miles in a west-north westerly direction to the Rameswaram Island (Latitude 9° 04' N. Longitude 79° 47' E.) and the Rameswaram Island which nearly joins the Indian coast. Its extreme width between Point-de-galle, the south-western point of Ceylon and Cape Comorin, the southern extreme of India, north-westward is about 204 miles.

The following places in the Gulf of Manar deserves special notice.

Kundugal Point—(Also known as Kuttikkal Point earlier):—It is a low sandy point with coconut plantations at a short distance inland. It extends northward and north-eastward and a beacon stands on the spot which extends about 1½ cables southward of Kundugal point. Tradition has it that *Hanuman* of the epic *Ramayana* sat on his calf muscles and leaped to Lanka in the fashion called "Kundugal" ([illegible]) in Tamil. This point and the channel are named after this incident. The tidal stream sets through Kundugal channel in a westerly direction with the flood tide, and from thence westward along the northern edge of the reef on which are Pamurichan Theevu and Kurusadi Theevu, (Latitude 9° 15' N. Longitude 79° 13' E.) where it meets the flood tidal streams setting in a north-westerly direction through Puma channel, these streams then combine and set in a northerly direction, but they are weak unless influenced by strong southerly winds.

There is a large coral reef, the western extreme of which is situated about 11½ miles west-south-westward of Kundugal point. On it are Musal Theevu, the south eastern point of which is about 10½ miles, west-south-westward of Kundugal point, and Manalai (Mannali Islet) about 2½ miles east-north-eastward of the south-eastern point of Musal Theevu. A white beacon 15 feet high stands on the reef about one cable eastward of Manali Theevu.

There is a coral reef, the western end of which is situated about 3 miles east-north eastward of Manali Theevu. The northern edge of this reef is clearly defined at low water, but its southern edge is much indented, and the sea breaks on it.

[illegible]

The region where the Kurusadi Island is situated is at the head of the Gulf of Manar. Here the water of the Gulf of Manar and the Palk Bay mix through the Palk Strait and the Pamban Pass. Here again southerly currents of low salinity enters the Gulf during the north-east monsoon period. Hydrographical observations made, therefore, by the Kurusadi Biological Station are doubtless of peculiar interest and inherent importance.

The well known Rameswaram Island is connected with the mainland by a bridge known as Pamban Bridge connecting the village Mandapam on the mainland and the hamlet of Pamban on the other side. A walk of 3½ miles in the southerly direction from Pamban leads to an abutting point of Rameswaram Island which is known as Kundugal point (Kuttikkal point by earlier works). The local people have a general faith about this place that it is from here that *Hanuman* of Ramayana jumped to Lanka (Ceylon). From this *Kundugal* ([illegible]) point, the Kurusadi Island is separated by a channel of about 250 metres in breadth. The pass of channel between Kurusadi and Kundugal point is popularly known as Kundugal channel. Its maximum depth is 20 feet with sandy bottom. The third oyster park of the station was first established in this Kundugal channel and it is being continued. In this channel water changes often during the day. On account of the changes in water current and in hydrographical condition, the appearance of myco organism and other animals varies. This channel is selected as suitable place for pearl oyster cultivation and the same is continued from 1929.

Every year a number of student parties sponsored by colleges visit the island. Usually they are biologists. They come and stay two or three days and study the biological organisms in the living condition in the natural environment. For their stay, two rest houses and a kitchen are provided. A motor launch is available at this station for hire for the convenience of students who visit the Island.

The Research Programme of work allotted for the year 1964-65 are as follows :—

1. Cultivation of sea-weeds in the Marine Fish Farm.
2. Meteorology and hydrology of Kundugal channel.
3. Pearl oyster farming in Kundugal channel.
4. Transplantation of pearl oysters at Calexea reef from Tuticorin.
5. Chank marking experiments at Ramanathapuram Coast.
6. Study of the bionomics of the fish captured at the inshore fishing station, Rameswaram.

Adam's Bridge.—The name "Adam's Bridge" is derived from the Muhammadan tradition that Adam on his expulsion from the paradise, crossed to Ceylon by this bridge. In Tamil it is called

[illegible]

Thiruvanai meaning Holy Bund. Its Sanskrit name is *Nalasethu* meaning *Nala* the monkey. *Sethu* the causeway or bund. It is also called Ramasethu meaning *Rama's* Bund. There is also another name, *Adisethu* meaning first bridge. It is situated at a distance of 112 miles in the east—south-east direction from Madurai and from Ramanathapuram it is 43 miles in the same direction. From Rameswaram it is 15½ miles to the east. It is a bridge of sand and rock mostly dry, nearly closing the Gulf of Manar on the north and north-east. Its western extremity joins the eastern point of Rameswaram Island and eastern extremity joins the eastern point of Manar Island. With these 2 islands, it almost connects Ceylon with the Peninsula. It is also called the bridge of Rama as *Rama* aided by *Hanuman* with his host of monkeys marched along it when invading Ceylon. This bridge connected Ceylon and India until 1480, when a breach was made in it by a ferocious storm. A subsequent storm enlarged this breach and foot traffic then ceased. Its length is about 30 miles and breadth is 1½ miles. It lies in the direction of south-east to north-west. This sand ridge is partly above and partly below water; but when covered it has about 3 or 4 feet of water. It is mostly composed of shifting sand banks with intricate channels between them. During south-west monsoon a strong current sets northward over Adam's bridge; a confused sea, which weakens to the westward as the Indian coast is approached. There is a proposal to cut a Channel across Adam's Bridge to connect the Gulf of Manar with the Palk Bay in order to shorten and improve the sea route between the west and the east coasts of India.

Mahibalanpatty (Tiruppattur Taluk—Population 1,976) lie 6 miles north-west of Tiruppattur and 18 miles west of Karaikkudi. Karaikkudi is the nearest railway station. This place is connected to Tiruppattur by a bus service.

A king by name *Mahibalan* was said to be ruling over this area and the village come to be named after this legendary king. The original name of the place is said to be Poongundram. The name was changed into Mahibalapatty during the period of the Chola kings.

This place was the capital of Poongundra Nadu, comprising 24½ villages, one of the divisions in Pandya kingdom. There is a tiny hillock in which a rock-cut *Siva* temple of the Pallava period exists with some inscriptions. The big *Lingam* is also a part of the rock-cut temple. By the side of it a *Valampuri Vinayagar* is cut on the rock, a little north to the rock-cut temple.

There are a number of temples in the village; *Poongundra-Nayakiamman* temple, *Vinayagar* temple, *Mangala Vinayagar* temple, *Nallamayyanar* temple, etc.

Relevant pages from the Gazette

Such published data, in this Gazette and other similar records, helps us today to build an authentic credible picture on the historicity of Rama and the construction of their bridge, Nala *Setu.*

Remote Sensing Agency Publication

The National Remote Sensing Agency, a unit of the department of Space, Government of India, has released its book, **"Images India"** based on the satellite mapping it has conducted. In this book, in the Chapter *"Stunning Structures"*, along with the NRSA image of the Adam's Bridge they state,

> *Satellite images have revealed*
> *an ancient bridge between*
> *India and Sri Lanka in the Palk Strait."*
>
> *"Its structure suggests that it may be man-made"*
>
> *"This 30 km long bridge, named as Adam's bridge,*
> *is made of a chain of shoals*
> *and links Rameshwaram in the South India to Sri Lanka."*
>
> *"This has an echo in the ancient Indian mythological epic,*
> *the Ramayana.*
> *According to the epic,*
> *such a bridge was built by Lord Rama*
> *and his followers to reach Sri Lanka.*
>
> *Studies are still on but the bridge is seen as an example*
> *of ancient history linked to the Indian mythology."*

Tourism Department Poster

The tourism department of the state of Tamil Nadu, in South India, on its part, regularly releases posters of the various tourist spots in the state of Tamil Nadu that could be visited by tourists from all over.

In one such poster, they invite one and all to come to Rameswaram to view the bridge constructed by the *Vanara* Team, which can be seen there even to this day.

We see here, the Tamil Nadu Government, as well the Government of India, through its various documents, have not only accepted the fact of Rama *Setu* being a constructed bridge in history, but have also established it through their own Government records.

ENCYCLOPAEDIA

ENCYCLOPÆDIA BRITANNICA online
Sharing knowledge since 1768

Encyclopaedia Brtiannica in their note on this bridge, also acknowledge the association of this bridge with Rama. This note reads as,

"Adam's Bridge also called Rama's Bridge, chain of shoals, between the islands of Mannar, near northwestern Sri Lanka and Rameswaram, off the southeastern coast of India. The bridge is 30 miles - 48 km, long and separates the Gulf of Mannar - southwest, from the Palk Strait - northeast. Some of the sandbanks are dry, and nowhere are the shoals deeper than 4 feet - 1 m.

Geologic evidence suggests that Adam's Bridge represents a former land connection between India and Sri Lanka. Traditionally, it is said to be the remnant of a huge causeway constructed by Rama, the hero of the Hindu epic Ramayana to facilitate the passage of his army from India to Ceylon - Sri Lanka, for the rescue of his abducted wife, Sita.

According to Muslim legend, Adam crossed there to Adam's peak, Ceylon, atop which he stood repentant on 1 foot for 1,000 years."

Nala *Setu* To Adam's Bridge

HOW DID THE NAME CHANGE?

The Sri Lankan Muslims named this bridge after *Aadhaam,* because their first Islamic leader walked over this bridge by foot from India to Lanka and thus this bridge has a holy connotation for them.

When the Europeans conquered Sri Lanka, since the name *Aadhaam* was easy on their tongue and had a similar meaning of Adam, it popularly came to be called Adam's Bridge, by the Europeans too.

But going back a few thousand years, Rama after winning over Ravana in a battle and rescuing Sita, flew back to Ayodhya, in the *Pushpaka Vimana.* During this flight, Rama pointed out this bridge to Sita as Nala *Setu* and explained to her that it was the bridge they had used to cross over to Lanka to battle with Ravana. Rama further explained how the construction of this bridge was very difficult and was finally possible due to the ingenuity and the engineering skill of Nala, owing to which Rama formally gave a name to this bridge as Nala *Setu,* to honour Nala's contribution.

Later, the people due to their adoration for Rama, called this bridge as Rama *Setu.*

Further later, people started calling it as *Setu Bandha,* meaning that which joins two lands.

Aadam, early Islamic leader crossed over to Lanka

That is how this bridge got its names, Nala *Setu,* Rama *Setu, Setu Bandha* and Adam's bridge.

ONE BRIDGE, MANY NAMES

Saraswati Mahal Library of Madras Presidency, British Raj 1803

One bridge with many names through its history of over 7100 years is but a natural fact for anything so ancient.

Is there any authentic proof for this?

The Saraswati Mahal Library of Thanjavur in the state of Tamil Nadu, is one of the premier libraries which has a repository of information on the colonial period. The Gazette entry, under Adam's Bridge, it reads as,

"Mohammedans called this bridge after Adam, who came down here after being expelled from the heaven and went to Ceylone using this bridge".

The Grand Convergence

Our examination of the historicity of Rama from various fields of arts and sciences, yields the following finds.

LITERATURE

We find that from the field of literature, Rama and the events of Ramayana have been considered historical, right from

- the Mahabharatha period 5000 years ago to
- the Tamil *Sangam* period between 5000 BCE to 400 CE to
- the period of invasions from the Northwest around 1000 CE to
- the Moghul period in India until 1600s and
- even during the initial visits of the Europeans upto 1800 CE

It is only after 1813 CE, when the History of India was written by the British, from their perspective, that it introduced the notion of mythology for these events and the persons who lived then.

GEOGRAPHY

There are over 500 sites in India as well as around 50 sites in Sri Lanka which claim a link to the events of Ramayana. We have looked at a few sites of India here. Some of the sites from the Sri Lankan side, as well as, a look at the events of Ramayana and Ravana from the Sri Lankan perspective, have been covered by us, in a separate book titled **"Ramayana In Lanka".**

Walking these trails, we find that not only do the names of these places, including some remote villages, off the beaten track, tally with the places as mentioned in the Ramayana, but their location, the terrain, topography, local folk lore, the tradition and practices that continue in those places even today, match with what the epic has to say in many places.

Some of the locations and the events that are said to have taken place there, also tally with the location as indicated for the skies and astronomical configurations mentioned in the Ramayana. Meaning, such observations could have been possible only from those locations, for the dates arrived at, based on the astronomical data in the Ramayana, thus making both the dates and the locale match in a water tight manner.

ARCHAEO-ASTRONOMY

The examination of the astronomical data available in the Ramayana and the exercise of recreating the skies when such astronomical configurations could have occurred, using highly advanced software called Planetarium software, provides us with dates for the events of Ramayana, as around 7000 years ago, around 5100 BCE.

These dates have been found to be consistent with the sequence of the events as per the text, as well as, the elapse time between each of the events, to the exact number of days.

This level of internal consistency, coupled with the fact, that the skies, as described in the text for certain events, match with the skies for those dates, as would have been visible from the locations as mentioned in the text too, lends even more credibility to these dates and the technique of dating.

ARCHAEOLOGY

We have seen how in a continuous civilization, it is difficult to find archaeological remains of a civilization over 7000 years old, especially on land or in inhabited places. Only remains, if any, in places deserted by mankind and left undisturbed by elements of nature, can provide the vital archaeological clues.

So far, the oldest structures of a bygone era that have been uncovered, are the Saqqara pyramids of Egypt, which date back to 4500 years ago, as they were left deserted in the deserts of Egypt.

Likewise, an only possible remain, from the period of Rama, could be the Nala *Setu* or Adam's Bridge of today, submerged in the seas, as we have seen. The possibility of the Adam's bridge being the man made Nala *Setu* of Rama's times seems to get vindicated by the tallying of the description of the location, construction as well as site conditions of the Nala *Setu* from the Ramayana text, with that of the Adam's Bridge of today.

Another factor which not only corroborates the convergence of Nala *Setu* with Adam's bridge, but also corroborates its age, is the Sea Level Rise factor.

Sea level rise

The sea levels keep rising and going down, based on various factors such as global warming, melting of ice caps and such others factors. 7000 years ago, during the times of Ramayana, when this bridge was built by the *Vanara* army, the sea level may not have been at the same level, as it is today.

Today this bridge is about 2 meters or 6 feet below the sea level. When the bridge was built by the *Vanara* team about 7000 years ago, it must have been about 1 meter or 3 feet above the then sea level. Therefore, the sea level when the bridge was built, must have been 3 metres or 9 feet lower than what it is today.

Sea level when the bridge must have built – 1 m or 3 feet below bridge

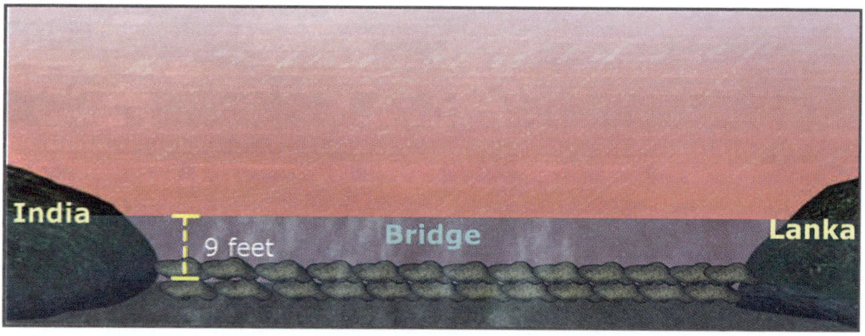

Sea level today - 6 feet above bridge or 9 feet rise totally

What do the world oceanography reports say of the sea levels 7000 years ago?

Discussions with various experts have revealed that based on the pattern of coral growth and the general trend of sea level rise for this region between the South Indian coast and Sri Lanka, the sea levels had been rising at the rate of 0.2 mm about 7000 years ago and later, the speed of sea level rise, increased progressively to 0.4 mm per year, then 0.6 mm per year, then to 0.8 mm a year, and later to 1.0 mm a year, to average out to 1.29 mm per year in recent times.

All these miniscule increases, cumulatively add upto 9.0 feet or about 3 metres, over the last 7000 years. Thus around 7000 years Before Present (BP), the sea level at the coast of Rameswaram could well have been around 3m or 9 feet lower.

Sea Level rise for the Holocene period i.e., from 12000 BP or 12000 years ago, across various regions also show an average rise of around 3m or 9 feet, from 7000 years ago or 7000 BP.

More details on this can be gathered from reports and charts published by Fleming et al. 1998, Fleming 2000, & Milne et al. 2005.

This approximate period of 7000 years, for the sea level in this region to have risen by 9 feet, obtained from the World Oceanography Studies, tallies well with the age of the Bridge that has been dated through Archaeo-Astronomy, as having been constructed 7000 years ago.

SUMMING UP

An integrated analysis of the above material in a rational, scientific and holistic manner confirms the following:

- Rama indeed was historical and should have lived 7200 years ago
- Rama and his team built a bridge across the seas to cross over to Lanka
- This bridge was named Nala *Setu* by Rama
- This bridge is a man made accretion over a natural sea ridge
- The upper surface of the bridge underwater, today is flat and levelled even today. This gives a greater degree of confidence, that it is manmade. If it were a natural surface, then it would be jagged and undulating in places and not so uniformly levelled.
- There are continuous records that talk about its usage until 1480 CE
- The bridge went into disrepair due to a cyclone in 1480 CE
- It was called the bridge of *Aadhaam* because Sri Lanka's first Muslim leader came to Sri Lanka from India over this Bridge
- The Europeans later found it easy to call it Adam's Bridge instead of Nala *Setu* or Rama *Setu*

- The Tamils in India, till the days of the poet *Maha Kavi* Subramania Bharathi, circa 1920 CE, have always cherished a dream of repairing the *Setu* and building a road to Sri Lanka
- The bridge has always been a protected monument for the Indians right through history from Mahabharatha times i.e., about 5000 years ago
- The Ramayana was classified as an *Itihasa* - historical text, until the perception was changed to "mythology" by British Historians in 1813 CE.

A TWIST IN THE TAIL

The Adam's Bridge or Nala *Setu* or Rama *Setu* which seems to be the only archaeological remains from Rama's times was designed by Nala, a qualified engineer of those times, trained through the education systems of learning of those days and built by the *Vanara*. Nala and the *Vanara* were residents of Kishkinda which is today known as Hampi in the south Indian state of Karnataka.

The southern part of India, lying on the southern side of the Vindhya mountain ranges, stretching from parts of present day state of Maharashtra on the West to parts of present day state of Orissa on the East, is known as Dravida land, in traditional geography.

Thus Nala and the *Vanara* were inhabitants of the Dravida land, making them the original Dravida or *Adi Dravida.*

The Rama *Setu* or Nala *Setu* thus symbolizes a feat of ancient *Adi Dravida* engineering.

It is to be noted that reference to Dravida land here, does not denote "the land of the Dravidian race". It denotes the geographical name given to this part of the land in ancient history and tradition.

It is an irony indeed, that this geographical classification took on a turn of racial classification and divided the people of India into Aryans belonging to north India and Dravidians belonging to South India.

Recent genetic studies have confirmed that all Indians, irrespective of whether they are from the north or the south, despite their distinctive features, skin colour, food habits and language, belong to the same race.

Recent, integrated historical studies by Indian as well as western historians have also negated the earlier theory of the invasion of India by the Aryans from the West and the movement of the Dravidians, the so called, original inhabitants of India, from North India to South India.

The theory of Aryan invasion stands debunked in the eyes of the historians of the scientific modern world.

Thus *Adi Dravida* engineering here, stands for the engineering skills prevalent in the geographical region known as Dravida, in the ancient days.

This name, Dravida, for the geographical region, south of the Vindhyas, finds a mention in the following lines of the National Anthem of India even today –

"... Punjab, Sind, Gujarat, Maratha,

Dravida, Utkala, Banga..."

THE CONVERGING VIEW OF RAMA

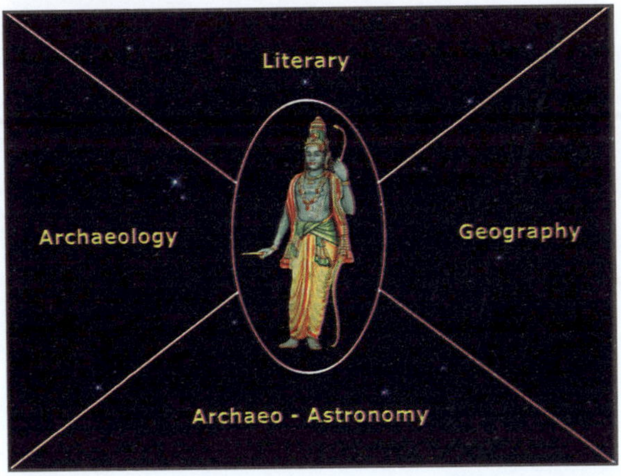

Thus from all angles we find that the events mentioned in the epic Ramayana have happened for real and have happened around 7000 years ago around 5100 BCE.

Rama is indeed historical and Ramayana, is one of the history books of this land.

Celebrating Our Heritage

Given the understanding that we have now, of the oldest man made structure of the world with us, what should be the next steps forward, to celebrate this heritage?

WORLD HERITAGE STATUS FOR NALA *SETU*

An ariel view of Nala *Setu*

Professor Malcom PR Right, of London University, has this to say on the bridge after studying it.

London University

"Adam's Bridge causeway must have been a major engineering feat, for its thin trace is still so clearly visible in the present day satellite images. It has resisted the relentless sea erosion and it attests to the great engineering skills of the ancient Indian people. It is the earliest and largest carbon-fibre reinforced civil engineering structure known to mankind and which needs to be protected as a world heritage site."

How did this bridge get the carbon fibre reinforcing?

If we recollect back, we have information in the Ramayana text, that wood was used in the base for cushion effect. Over the 7000 years period, under the sea, this wood would have solidified and become carbonaceous material. Probably this is what Professor Malcom Right is referring to, when he mentions that the bridge is a carbon fibre reinforced engineering structure.

This clear a statement, gives us the confidence, that we have the earliest carbon reinforced civil engineering structure, which we need to showcase and display to all, as a heritage structure.

SELECTION CRITERIA FOR A HERITAGE SITE

As per the Archaeological Survey of India Act, Clause (iv), for anything to be declared as a heritage monument, it has

"to be an outstanding example of a type of building, architectural or technological ensemble or landscape which illustrates a significant state in human history"

Again, as per the Ancient Monuments and Archaeological Sites and Remains Act, 1958, 58 (b) *"antiquity"* includes-

- *any article, object or thing illustrative of science, art, crafts, literature, religion, customs, morals or politics in bygone ages,*
- *any article, object or thing of historical interest,*

Given the range of history and recognition behind it, the Nala *Setu* bridge is a fit case to be recognized as a Heritage Monument, under these clauses as the bridge qualifies under each one of them,

- as a structure that has found mention in literature of many thousand years old,
- with the historicity of Rama, it also becomes a structure of historical interest to both India and Sri Lanka.

It presents itself as not only a Heritage Monument, but also as

- A civil engineering marvel,
- The oldest surviving structure of the world and
- An underwater monument.

Also given that such considered opinions exist among the experts of the world, we need to now rightfully promulgate an order declaring the Nala *Setu* as a Heritage Monument.

The story, history and structure of this bridge make it also appropriate to appeal to suitable World bodies for conferring World Heritage Status on the Nala *Setu*.

ENSUING IMPLICATIONS

What would such a status and recognition for the bridge bring about?

Today the largest and oldest manmade structure is generally considered to be the Pyramids of Egypt. These draw worldwide attention and hordes of tourists to come there, to relish its engineering and aesthetics, as well as soak in all the history and mystery that surround these structures.

Similarly this bridge, as an older civil engineering marvel, could bring hordes of tourists from the world over, apart from the trickle of regular pilgrims today.

When this bridge is researched right, projected right and given the right tourist facilities around it such as hotels, airports, glass bottom boats and the likes, it can give a boost to the local economy of the regions on both ends of the bridge.

With time it can perhaps also pave the way for a land route and closer ties, between the 2 lands of India and Sri Lanka once again.

Questions Galore

The historicity of Rama, the dates for Rama and events of Ramayana, give India a 7000 year old, authentic recorded history. The restoration of the classification of the legend from a myth to history, will now reopen a number of questions in connection with various descriptions and events that were easy to dismiss as a myth earlier but are difficult to answer from the perspective of present day science and knowledge.

These open a lot of vistas for future research on this subject from a rational, logical and wholistic perspective.

DATE OF RAMAYANA – 300 BCE OR BEFORE?

Valmiki
the *Adi Kavi* Episode

Certain literary analysts have placed the Valmiki Ramayana to be of the period of 300 BCE based on the style of the language. How do you then place the events of Ramayana to be around 5000 BCE?

Valmiki is considered to be the first poet, *Adi Kavi* of the Samskrt language.

The European colonial scholars had dated the Valmiki Ramayana text to 300 BCE because they then had to fit all the literature of India and its history, well within 1200 BCE. This date was sacrosanct for the European historians, because they had fixed the time of the Aryan invasion as 1500 BCE.

According to this Aryan Invasion theory, Indians were a barbaric civilization and were only made civilized by the Aryans who came to India from the North West of India or Central parts of Europe. Hence, India before this period, could not have had kings and rich kingdoms with learned scholars, poets etc. and no good literature could have come from India before that period.

The Aryan invasion theory has recently been debunked by the rest of the world, based on scientific grounds. But the thoughts around the Aryan Invasion are yet to be erased from the Indian minds even today.

In the last 5 decades of research, this upper cap of 1200 BCE as the start for culture, literature and progress in India, has been rightfully dismissed based on ground facts, arrived at, using modern scientific processes. This gives the present day analysts, the true flexibility of placing the text where it should naturally belong, in the timeline.

Their earlier assumption was that if the *Veda* were compiled in 1200 BCE, then Panini must have lived around 500 BCE. A group of literary analysts, because of the style of writing had opined that since the Ramayana narration style is in line with the Paninian grammar, the Ramayana must have been composed post Panini, somewhere around 300 BCE.

Panini-The Grammarian

The events of Ramayana and the lifetime of Rama therefore were also placed around 300 BCE.

Due to this, India and her ancient culture were reduced to a mere two thousand years. Even to this day, 300 BCE is still used by many international historians and researchers as a historical milestone for India and we find that, in many western works, which compare the ancient cultures of the world, Indian history is wrongly placed much after the Egyptians and the Mayans.

The danger lying in this is that, it can lead to a grossly wrong picture of the evolution of mankind globally.

It has now been proved that the *Veda* were not compiled in 1200 BCE, but were infact compiled well before 3000 BCE i.e., about 5000 years ago. The events of Mahabharatha, that succeeded much after Ramayana, also have been conclusively dated to 3100 BCE or 5100 years ago.

Given this, the date of Panini also needs to be looked at afresh and fixed accordingly, as also the many other dates in Indian history.

Assignment of a specific date to a text and hence dating of the events mentioned in that text, purely based only on analysis of the "literary style" of the language by a few literary analysts, can at best be termed, as a soft evidence.

Whereas, in contrast, dating the events in a text using the hard evidences in the form of "content in the text", which tallies and cross verifies with scientific finds and other texts and legends, across times, is a much more reliable method.

Looking at it from this hard evidence perspective, 5114 BCE as the date for Rama and the events in Ramayana seems to be a more reliable date.

WRITTEN OR ORAL TRADITION IN INDIA?

We are told that, in India, an oral tradition of knowledge transmission was followed. If so, how can we rely on this written text as containing authentic data?

It is only the *Veda*, known as *Shruti*, that were meant to be orally transmitted. *Shruti* means to listen. They were never intended to be written down.

Veda contain the ancient knowledgebase. The ancient Indians had concluded that oral transmission was more effective than physical media for transmission of this knowledge. Various error correcting transmission techniques were therefore put in place to ensure the correctness of this transmission of knowledge.

Veda* Oral Transmission – *Shruti

In contrast, the 2 *Itihasa,* historical texts, namely the Ramayana and the Mahabharatha were texts which were written down and copied through the ages, in different media, through the land, as it continues to happen even today for our current texts.

From this, what comes out is that, minor additions and deletions could have and have taken place in various versions of these texts across the land. On close scrutiny of the different versions we find that, the core data however is the same across these versions and we can sift out the additions and localizations.

WHY SO MANY RAMAYANA?

The various Ramayana texts across the ages, can be termed as versions, editions and adaptations.

In order to keep the history alive, the original Valmiki Ramayana was copied into newer manuscripts or other textual forms, every few hundred years. Over time, different chroniclers of the Ramayana text, have woven their own interpretation, language and style, in their respective edition of the Ramayana text as interpolations to the original text, without destroying the original, main details.

These can be called as editions.

Ramayana as a story has and continues to inspire and move many.

Hence many other authors have commented and rewritten the legend based on how they have understood the facts of the core data in their times and how they have wanted to present it to their societies, in tune with the times of their days. These could be called versions of the Ramayana.

Even today, we have many writers, writing their own version of the Ramayana, in the languages spoken today, using computers as a medium for typing and books as a medium for publishing.

Besides these, many distinguished poets, saints and religious leaders across the times have also created adaptations of the original Valmiki Ramayana in the form of ballads, plays and religious texts such as Kalidasa's *Raghuvamsha,* Tulsidas' *Ram Charit Manas* and Kambar's *Tamil Ramayana.*

We thus find today, multiple adaptations, versions and editions of the Ramayana, both in India as well as across South East Asia.

WHICH IS THE ORIGINAL TEXT?

The question then is, which do we use as the authentic text?

Firstly, it is important to note that across all these adaptations, versions or editions, the focus and purpose of each of the authors of these works was different and the social conditions of their times have found expression too, in the message conveyed through their works.

While Valmiki Ramayana is the original epic, we have already seen that there have been various editions, as this text has been handed down across generations. Secondly we have also seen that there are various adaptations of this original text too.

Hence, while embarking on a scientific or historic research of such an ancient civilization with such a vast amount of literature, it is essential to scan through the variety of versions and adaptations and gather the common, credible, core data to analyze and appreciate the historicity of Rama.

WERE HANUMAN AND THE *VANARA*, MONKEYS?

How do we explain the monkeys in Ramayana? If Rama was historical, how could people of those time converse with monkeys?

Vanara **- Hanuman**

Monkey is a term that has been loosely used in the last couple of hundred years to explain the term *Vanara* in the English language. The term *Vanara* when analyzed, can give us vital suggestive clues, some of them being:

- People of the forest or *Vana –Vana nara*
- *Vanara* could be an exclamatory ! word as in *"Are they human too?" Vah nara?* So human like, yet so different !

This may have been the way to express different varieties of people as is evident from other words in our ancient texts such as *Kinnara* or *Kimpurusha* too. *Kin, Kim* here meaning, *"Are they?"* and *Purusha* and *Nara* meaning men or humans.

So there probably were some people in those days, very similar to what we now understand as normal humans, but who had a minor perceptible variance, which raised exclamation. This could well have been a part of the evolution process.

The word Hanuman has an etymological root in the Samskrt language, meaning, "one with the long jaw". Anjaneya is another name for Hanuman, meaning son of Anjana, who was the mother of Hanuman. Anjaneya had a long protruding jaw and hence got the name Hanuman too.

It is interesting to note here that, in the British records of the Gazette of Bellary district, which is very near modern day Hampi, i.e., Kishkinda of earlier times, the then collector has noted that the forest tribes of that area, call themselves the *Vanara* people and used Monkey as a symbol in their totem pole and flag. Kishkinda was the land of the *Vanara* in the Ramayana text. So, perhaps monkey was the emblem of the *Vanara* of those times too, which possibly led to them being referred to as Monkeys and subsequent imagery only reinforced the same.

***Vanara* Totem pole Flag**

The Fast Paced Evolution

The concept of evolution has been in vogue in modern thinking for the past 200 years since the writings of Charles Darwin on the subject of evolution. In India, the concept of evolution has been understood and discussed in the sequence of *Dasavatara* of Vishnu, starting from the fish and evolving all the way to the intellectual human. This process and concept in the Indian texts is known as *Parinama.*

This parallel thought and the process, we shall discuss in one of our future works in the Bharath Gyan Series. What is relevant to the legend of Ramayana is where, Rama and many others are described as fully evolved humans, while the *Vanara* are described to have monkey like features.

How is this possible? Is it not an enigma that 2 species, in the stages of human evolution, seem to have lived in the same period, conversed and interacted with one another in a conducive manner?

Evolution stages from monkey to human are said to take lakhs and millions of years. If the events of Ramayana happened only 7000 years ago, then how is it that an earlier form of man, in an evolution process that happens over a very long time span, could have lived just 7000 years ago?

A Monumental Genetic Change in 1000 years

While the theory that evolution needs lakhs and millions of years is more than a few decades old, the newer theories speak of the process of evolution, not necessarily requiring such very long time spans, but in fact some aspects of the evolutionary process happening in small time spans of 10000 years and less.

Dr. Oliver Curry, Lead researcher, London School of Economics, says,

"Over the subsequent millennia, due to an over reliance on technology reducing our natural capacity to resist diseases or our evolved ability to get along with each other, a monumental genetic change over can be expected."

"Men will have symmetrical facial features, deep voices and bigger penises while women will all have glossy hair, smooth hairless skin, wide eyes and pert breasts."

"Reliance on technology will dramatically change the appearance of the human race."

"Humans will evolve into 2 species –

- *an attractive, intelligent, ruling elite*
- *an underclass of dim witted ugly goblin like creatures.*

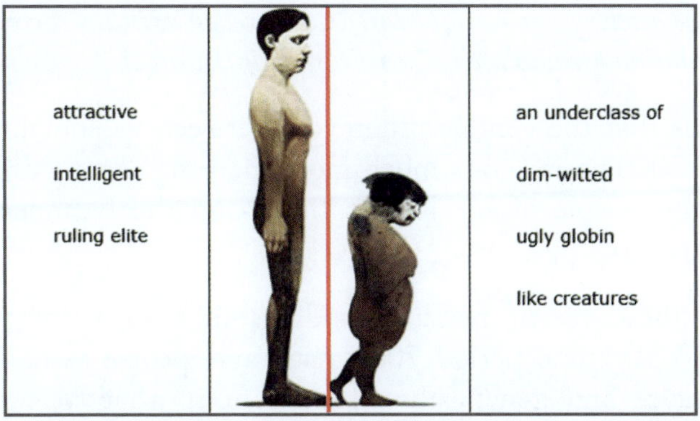

An illustration of the 2 human species 1000 years hence

Humans will evolve in the next 1000 years into giants between 6 feet and 7 feet tall, while life spans will have extended to 120 years.

Human race would reach its physical peak by the year 3000."

Colossal Population Growth and Evolutionary Impacts

Dr.Henry Harpending, Anthropologist in University of Utah, summarizes his findings as,

"The central finding is that human evolution is happening very fast – faster than any of us thought."

He says that the changes have been driven by the colossal growth in population from a few million to 6.5 billion in 10000 years, with people moving to new environments to which they need to adapt.

Accelerated Genetic Differences

Dr. John Hawks, Anthropologist at the University of Wisconsin, in the Research Journal Proceedings of the National Academy of Sciences, says,

"People today are genetically more different from those living 5000 years than those humans were different from the Neanderthals, who vanished 30000 years ago."

"Most of the acceleration is in the last 10000 years, basically corresponding to the population growth after agriculture was invented."

This means that the genetic differences between us and the people who lived 5000 years ago is much more than the genetic differences between the people of say Rama's times and the Neanderthals of 30000 years ago.

From all these recent research findings, it does seem plausible that during the time period 7000 years ago, people were different in appearance and genetically different from what we are today. This time window could indeed have had people in different transitional stages of evolution, running into each other, since the lesser population was widely spread across the varied geographies of the world.

DID RAMA WALK THIS EARTH ONLY 7000 YEARS AGO?

As per the *Puranic* literature, Rama was born in *Treta Yuga.*

Now, does not the *Yuga* period run into lakhs and millions of years? Then how do we say that Rama lived only 7000 years ago and was born in 5114 BCE? What is the time span of a *Yuga* and how long ago was *Treta Yuga?*

Let us now look at what the word *Yuga* means.

The word *Yuga* is etymologically similar to the word *Yoga.* Both the word *Yoga* and *Yuga* mean *"to join"* and come from the root *Yug* or *Jug.* The English words yoke, join, have all come from the same etymological root.

Yoga is the union of body and mind.

Yuga is the alignment or conjunction in the sky, of the various stellar and planetary bodies.

So *Yuga* is not a particular time span that runs into lakhs of years but a generic term for the measure of time period between different alignments.

Yuga is a term that denotes only a scale of measure of time. There are many types of *Yuga* to measure various time spans. There are at least 7 types of *Yuga* periods of time, that have been mentioned in ancient treatises.

We have *Yuga* time spans ranging from 1 year to 5 years and extending all the way upto 4,320,000 years.

Every year when the Sun, Earth and Moon come in alignment with the Aries Zodiac, it is a *Yuga* and denotes the time span of a year and is celebrated as *Yugadi* or *Ugadi* i.e., New Year in the Indian states of Maharashtra, Karnataka and Andhra Pradesh. This means that, every year, when Sun, Earth and Moon come in alignment with a Zodiac, it is considered to be start of a new *Yuga* that is why it is called *Yuga-adi* or *Ugadi. Adi* means start or beginning.

Every 12 years when the Sun, Earth and Jupiter come in alignment it is a *Yuga.*

Every 60 years when the Sun, Earth and Jupiter, Saturn come in alignment it is a *Yuga.*

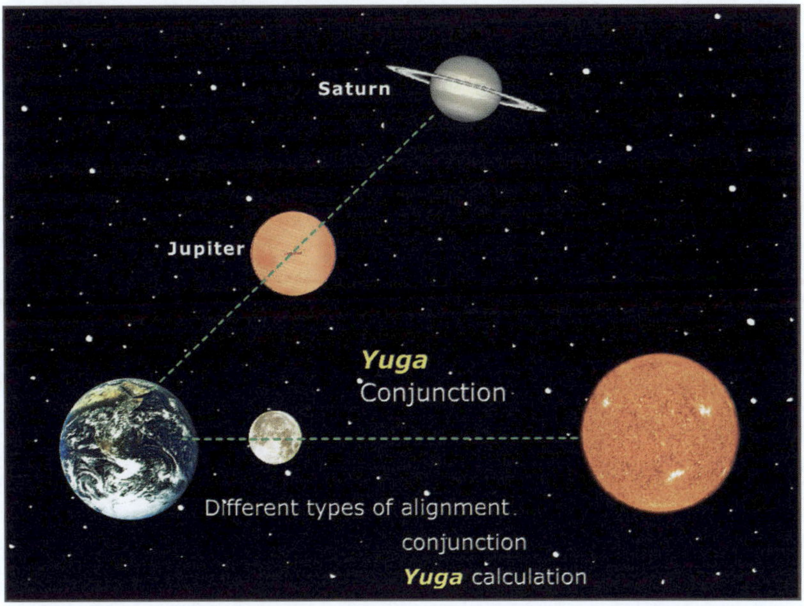

Different types of alignment, conjunction, *Yuga* calculation

Similarly, about 5100 years ago, on Friday, 18th February, 3102 BCE, at 02 hours, 30 minutes, 23 seconds to be precise, all the planets of the solar system were in alignment and this marked the start of the *Kali Yuga* which was an astronomical alignment.

There are seven prominent types of *Yuga.*

	Yuga	period in earth years
1.	*Sanskara*	4, 5, 12, 18, 19 in which education & other human based activities are achieved
2.	*Manava*	60, 100, 120 human life span
3.	*Parivarta*	360
4.	*Sahasra*	time taken for *saptha rishi* Ursa Major to rotate round the 27 *nakshathra*
5.	*Dhurva*	3 times sahasra yuga
6.	*Ayana*	Milankovitch cycle
7.	*Chathur*	43,20,000

Various Types of *Yuga*

So the span of *Yuga* starts all the way from one year period going all the way upto 43,20,000 years which is an astronomical *Yuga.* Each variety of *Yuga* is used as a measure for various purposes. The type of *Yuga* running into lakhs or millions of years is used to measure time periods for astronomical alignments at Solar System or Galactic levels. Lakh is a popular unit of measure in India. 1 Lakh = 100,000 and 10 Lakhs = 1 Million.

Similar is the case with the term *Yojana.* There are many varieties of *Yojana* for measuring different types of distances, such as *Bhu Yojana* for measuring distances on Earth scale, *Bha Yojana* for measuring distances with respect to the Sun, *Nara Yojana* for distances with respect to man etc.

Thus the term *Yojana* was more a generic unit of measure rather than a fixed measure. Also, these units varied from region to region as they were also based on local references. Hence with just the term *Yojana*, cannot always calculate absolute values for those measures.

Thus out of all these varieties of *Yuga* and their subdivisions, which *Yuga* span and which variety of *Treta Yuga* has been used in connection with Rama in the Ramayana text is unclear.

Moreover, the reference to *Treta Yuga* in the Ramayana text is only in the *Uttara Khanda,* the additional section and there too mentioned only indirectly. Many literary scholars consider this section to have been a later day inclusion in one of the editions, rather than from the original.

Given all this, we on our own, cannot imagine what Valmiki may have intended in his *Itihasa* and take for our calculation, only the Solar System *Yuga* span, of the seventh variety i.e., the astronomical *Yuga* period of 4,32,000 years and conclude that Rama must have lived several lakh or million years ago.

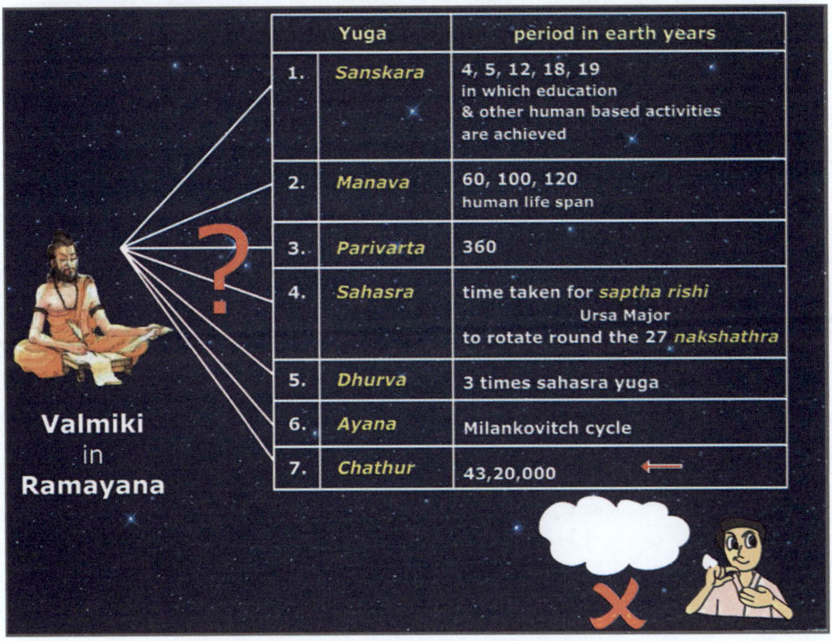

	Yuga	period in earth years
1.	Sanskara	4, 5, 12, 18, 19 in which education & other human based activities are achieved
2.	Manava	60, 100, 120 human life span
3.	Parivarta	360
4.	Sahasra	time taken for saptha rishi Ursa Major to rotate round the 27 nakshathra
5.	Dhurva	3 times sahasra yuga
6.	Ayana	Milankovitch cycle
7.	Chathur	43,20,000

***Treta Yuga* of Ramayana – Which of these?**

Given this state of affairs, if we look for a corroborative data in the various *Purana,* then we do find a description in the *Vayu Purana* which seems to fit into the 7000 year period for the lifetime of Rama.

The division of *Yuga,* as per *Vayu Purana,* is shown here.

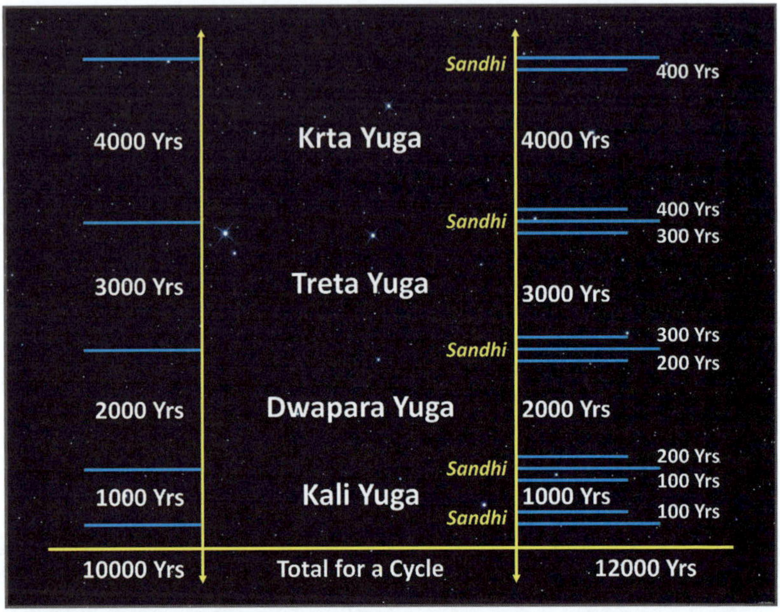

***Chathur Yuga* Cycle as per *Vayu Purana* – 32.58 - 64**

As per *Vayu Purana,* the *Yuga* cycle is of 10000 years with

- 4000 years for *Krta Yuga,*
- 3000 years for *Treta Yuga,*
- 2000 years for *Dwapara Yuga* and
- 1000 years for *Kali Yuga.*

At a finer level, it also specifies intermediate periods or *Sandhi* periods as shown in the chart, taking the whole cycle to be 12000 years.

There is also a mention in the *Vayu Purana* of an elapsed time gap of 2000 years between the end of *Treta Yuga* and the end of *Dwapara Yuga.*

Rama is inferred to have been born towards the end of *Treta Yuga.*

With 3102 BCE calculated as the end of *Dwapara Yuga* and the start of *Kali Yuga,* the calculation of year 5114 BCE or 7000 years ago, as the period for Rama and Ramayana using *Treta Yuga* from this scale, seems to fit in well with the other corroborating data from various other fields, that we have seen through this work.

The medieval western concept of time was linear. The Indian concept of time is cyclical. All the scales of time are concurrent. Therefore at the same moment, we can be described to be in different *Yuga,* as per different *Yuga* scales. It depends upon the context we are relating to and the scale of measurement. This is the key thought and distinction we have to realize. More on this can be found in our book "The Indian concept of Time", in the Bharath Gyan Series.

It is also to be borne in mind, that millions of years ago, the sky configurations, as well as Earth's geology and geography would have been very different from what it is now and what has been described in the text. Also mankind's history and memory cannot carry tales, legends, practices and tradition across millions of years, with such clarity and geographical details that seem to be valid even today.

All the above clearly bring forth a high degree of possibility for the events of Ramayana to have occurred around 5100 BCE.

WHAT ABOUT NASA'S COMMENTS ON THE AGE OF THE BRIDGE?

NASA's satellite images show the Adam's Bridge and based on that the bridge has been dated to be 1,750,000 years old.

So does not a date of 7000 years create a conflict with this time period as indicated by the NASA images?

When the photographs from NASA were released on the net, the date 1,750,000 years, for the land at the 2 ends of the bridge, tallied with the popular impression in people's mind, of millions of years for *Treta Yuga.* These photographs therefore suddenly kindled interest amongst Indians, who were looking for scientific proofs for the bridge constructed by Rama and His team.

These satellite pictures from NASA of the causeway, therefore started finding their way into email boxes of many Indians all over the globe, to the extent that this bridge and its shape have become popular knowledge today.

While NASA in their statement on these photographs have stated that the lands at both ends of the causeway are over 1.7 million years old, they also clarified that this age was deduced using geology, archaeology and other fields.

India, Sri Lanka connected by the bridge

They advised and cautioned that Satellite photography can at best be an additional tool in understanding the form of structures, but not for arriving at their age and that, other sources of information would have to be considered, to arrive at the age and composition of such structures.

We need to therefore judiciously look at the images and the original statements of NASA and draw a scientific understanding of what this bridge, causeway can mean.

There are three inferences we can draw from NASA's photograph and statements.

- The bridge, causeway has been identified as Adam's bridge.
- The time period mentioned therein of 1.7 million years is not specifically of the bridge, but of the two ends of the adjoining land.
- The shape of this structure, which has a unique curvature, suggests that it could be man made. It is not an emphatic statement, but only a suggestive view based on an observation.

Given the data available to us now from different fields and our awareness of the different types of *Yuga,* we can also use the satellite image as additional data, to understand the whole picture, from an inter-disciplinary perspective, which this subject rightfully deserves.

We cannot however conclude on the date or composition of the bridge structure based only on NASA's images.

WAS *PUSHPAKA VIMANA* REAL? DID RAMA & RAVANA REALLY FLY IN *VIMANA*?

What about the flying machines of the Ramayana period?

Vimana is the word for flying machines or aircrafts in the Samskrt language, as well as in many of the present day Indian languages.

There has been mention of a variety of *Vimana,* in the Indian literature.

Pushpaka Vimana of Ravana, in which Rama returned to Ayodhya from Lanka, after his victory over Ravana, was just one among the many *Vimana.* Ravana had many other *Vimana* which we discuss in our other work **"Ramayana In Lanka".**

While there are many stories in the *Purana* and in the epics Ramayana and Mahabharatha that speak about *Vimana,* there are separate, technical literature available such as *Vaimanika Sastra* by Maharishi Bharadwaja, which discuss the *Vimana* from a technical perspective.

In such technical texts, the avionics of these *Vimana* are discussed in great detail. In the Bharath Gyan Series, we have a separate capsule on *Vimana,* where we discuss and analyze the concept of *Vimana* in detail.

This text describes the design of a few aircrafts and discusses about the fuel, mechanisms and manoeuvres of the same.

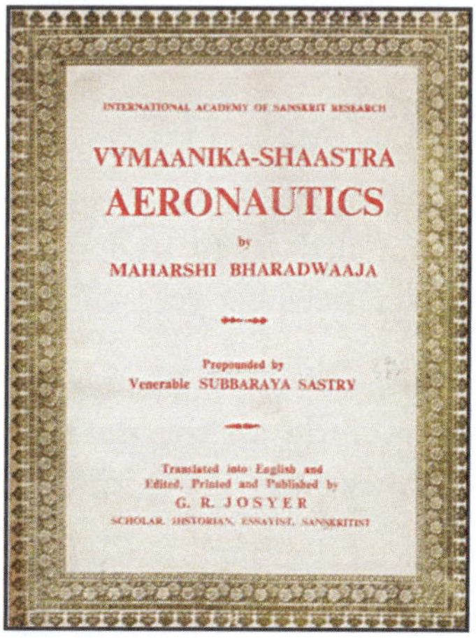
INTERNATIONAL ACADEMY OF SANSKRIT RESEARCH

VYMAANIKA-SHAASTRA

AERONAUTICS

by

MAHARSHI BHARADWAAJA

Propounded by
Venerable SUBBARAYA SASTRY

Translated into English and
Edited, Printed and Published by
G. R. JOSYER
SCHOLAR, HISTORIAN, ESSAYIST, SANSKRITIST

***Vaimanika Sastra* of Maharishi Bharadwaja**

Along with these, it also lists out the various *Vimana* in the different *Yuga.*

Vimana listed for Treta Yuga

Ambareesha	Panchaanana	Vajraanga
Archisah	Panchabaana	Varnapanchaka
Bheeshmaka	Pushpaka	Vasuhaara
Bherunda	Shankara priya	
Bhooshnu	Shanmukha	
Dyvata	Shesha	
Hraaja	Sommanka	
Jamukha	Swayamjyoti	
Kolaahala	Trinetra	
Kowshika	Tripura	
Mayoora	Ujvala	

Vimana* used in *Treta yuga

Here we see that *Pushpaka Vimana* is listed under *Treta Yuga*, the *Yuga* when Rama and Ravana lived, based on various references to the time period in the text. *Pushpaka Vimana* originally belonged to Kubera the step brother of Ravana. It was taken away by Ravana from Kubera and used by him to kidnap Sita.

Later after the victorious battle, where Rama defeated Ravana, Rama and Sita flew back to Ayodhya from Lanka in the *Pushpaka Vimana,* loaned to them by Vibhishana, who was crowned the King of Lanka, after Ravana's death at the hands of Rama.

Hanuman's *Vimana, Vajraanga* also finds a mention in this list of the *Vimana* of *Treta Yuga.*

It is indeed amazing to note that the names and characteristics of the *Vimana* across various stories in the different *Puranic* texts, tally well with each other, as also with the time period and capabilities of the *Vimana,* as mentioned in the technical texts.

As an interesting side point, it will be worthy of note that Rama who is considered as a Divine *Avatara,* God, could not fly on His own. He needed a mechanical flying machine, in this case *Pushpaka Vimana.*

Whereas, in contrast to this, Hanuman could fly across the seas.

Hanuman flying

Vibhishana, the brother of Ravana, when he differed with his brother, King Ravana, on principles of morality before the battle, flew across the sea from Lanka to the shores of India, to join sides with Rama.

Vibhishana flying

Surpanaka, the sister of Ravana, who suffered a nose cut in the hands of Lakshmana at Panchavati, Nasik, flew away from the scene, to her brothers, Khar and Dushan, after the incident.

Surpanaka flying

Another interesting point to note is that Ravana, the King of Lanka, too did not fly on his own and relied on a mechanical vehicle, a *Vimana* to fly.

How were some of these people such as Hanuman, Vibhishana, Surpanaka etc. able to fly at will, on their own, without a *Vimana?*

Some of the *Purana* also speak about Hanuman having a mechanical contrivance called *Vajranga.*

What could the *Vajranga* be?

Modern advancements in human short flight design technology, provide us with some clues.

Fusion Man

The Fusion Man project, initiative had 4 engines strapped to the back of a Swiss Military Pilot, the first to fly with such a device, in May 2008. This contraption can be seen at the International Exhibition of Inventions in Geneva.

Yves Rossy, the Swiss Military Pilot, had this to say after his flight *"It was absolutely fantastic – total freedom in three dimensions. So much speed and power, it is better than a bird".*

The Fusion Man Project

Flying Sheets

Prof. Lakshminarayanan Mahadevan, Professor and Lead Researcher, in Harvard School of Engineering and Applied Sciences, Cambridge, Massachussettes, who has done a lot of work on the aerodynamics of a rippling sheet, in his papers, published in the Journal, Physical Review of Letters, talks of an invention which would move in a way similar to sea creatures such as rays and skates, which have been known to breach and fly briefly above the water.

Wing Suits

Wing Suit is an invention that enables people to fly more like the flying squirrel than birds or airplanes. Physicists such as Dr. Jean Potvin from the Saint Louis University, remark that all of this is technically possible.

Maria von Egidy, a Wing Suit maker from South Africa is hoping for a reaction such as *"Why did not someone think of this long ago?"*

Wing suit

Jean Albert in wing suit

Jean Albert, a Wing Suit flier, says that Wing Suit totally changes the way one flies or jumps.

It opens up a third dimension in flying unlike normal sky diving where trajectories are pretty much only vertical.

Could the *Vajranga* of Hanuman, have been something like a Wing Suit?

To answer this question, as is the norm again, in the Samskrt language, we have to understand the etymology of the word *Vajranga.* This word may be split as *Vajra* and *Anga. Vajra* is associated with strength, hardness, diamond, power, source of energy etc. while *Anga* means part or an extension of the self.

Thus *Vajranga* conjures up an image of something which is strong, hard, source of power or energy and which is worn or is an extended part of the body. As a *Vimana,* it gives the ability to fly.

Very intriguing, indeed! Throws up many newer dimensions to the legends and heroes of lore!

More on the ancient *Vimana* from the perspective of Ravana and the Ramayana period has been covered in our book **"Ramayana in Lanka".**

BUT RAMA IS A GOD, SO HOW IS RAMA HISTORICAL?

While Rama has been revered right through the ages as a divinity, the people across generations have also believed the story of Ramayana to have been real and a record of history.

Even to this day, people across India and Sri Lanka, connect some of the places in their lands, with the events and people of Ramayana times and the names of people and places have continued to stay.

As we have seen from an integrated and wholistic perspective, the legend of the Ramayana is true and can be dated precisely, thus giving credence to the historicity of Rama.

While Historicity is a matter of existence, Divinity is a matter of faith.

Divinity and faith are aspects that far transcend the limits of understanding of history and sciences today.

Given this, the Historicity of Rama, does not in any way diminish the Divinity of Rama.

On the contrary, it can serve as a beautiful medium to bridge the gap between Sciences and Faith.

Rama – Historical and Divine

MANY MORE *YOJANA* TO GO...

What we have presented here are plausible answers to the numerous questions we have about Rama, Ramayana and those times. These are but just a tip of the iceberg. There are many more questions that remain to be probed and many more questions that these answers will further throw up.

These plausible answers have come our way, based on our digging further into the ancient knowledge and making note of the findings of present day advancements in science and technology.

Further research, taking cognizance of both ancient and modern knowledge, can perhaps yield more answers to the other questions.

Not only that, as quite a few aspects of the legends are turning out to be plausible and credible, there is a strong possibility of the remaining also being plausible and credible, as science keeps on discovering itself.

This thought also throws up a whole new vista for research where the technologies mentioned in the ancient texts can provide new impetus and ideas for further advancements in science and technology.

Conclusion

A MORAL HIGH GROUND

Today, the present world order, is unfortunately wanting in moral qualities.

When it comes to morality, honesty and good character, the name that comes uppermost to everyone's lips is Rama and next to that is the name of the historical personage, Mahatma Gandhi, who lived amongst us about 100 years ago.

While it has been easy for everyone to accept Gandhi as a historical role model, due to the close proximity of his times with ours, it has not been easy with Rama, due to the long gap between the times of Rama and ours and more also due to the notion of "mythology", attributed to Rama and Ramayana, as we have seen in this work.

The signs of the influence of Rama and Rama's Solar dynasty however, can be seen all the way from ancient Egypt where the Pharaohs took on the name Ramses, to Thailand, where the Kings, even today, are called Rama. The present King is Rama IX. The earlier capital of the Thailand kings was also called Ayuthaya.

Mahatma Gandhi, himself, when he fought against the oppressive colonialism, used the concepts of *"Rama Rajya"* or "the rule of Rama", to unshackle India from the British rule. This served as a role model for the rest of the nations, still fighting colonial oppression.

Rama – A Noble King

Mahatma Gandhi – Father of the Nation

Understanding the historicity of Rama and the events of Ramayana, along with the local customs, traditions and legends of the land, can offer us a better foundation for not only understanding the history of India but also for understanding the history of the world cultures and civilizations, from the perspective of the right timeline and spread.

With the restored belief in the historicity of Rama, perhaps the noble qualities of Rama, one of the noblest kings of this land and the principles of governance He advocated, may once again offer the moral beacon light, the world is looking for, to come out of its current imbroglio.

When History meets Tradition and

Tradition meets Science and

Science meets Nature,

Can we advance as truly mature peoples.

Epilogue

UNRAVELLING THE HISTORICITY OF RAMA

Only if Rama is a historical person and the events mentioned in the texts are historical, can the *Setu* bridge mentioned in the Ramayana, be a man made structure. Conversely, if the bridge is found to be manmade, then it can go to prove the historicity of Rama.

The historicity of both Rama and the Nala *Setu,* Rama *Setu* or Adam's Bridge go hand in hand and unravelling its details can change many a thing for India as well as world history and economics.

This compilation is a part of the Bharath Gyan effort of compiling specific, scientific information on the knowledge of India for well over 10 years, in 108 subjects, which may be viewed at our website www.bharathgyan.com or contact us at bharathgyan@gmail.com.

The research compilation has been made possible with the inputs given by many traditional scholars juxtaposed with the views of modern scientists.

The beauty and marvel of the whole endeavour is that all the individual aspects of the knowledge of India, fit in beautifully into a large jigsaw puzzle, which is India.